Hinduism and Judaism

ROBERT McVEIGH & JOE WALKER

Series Editor: Robert McVeigh

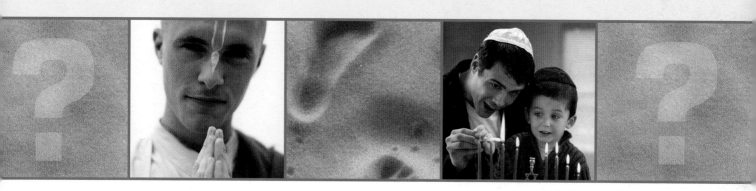

Hodder Gibson
A MEMBER OF THE HODDER HEADLINE GROUP

The Publishers would like to thank the following for permission to reproduce copyright material:
Photo credits CIRCA Photo Library / William Holtby (6), © ArkReligion.com / Alamy (7), CIRCA Photo Library/Bipin J. Mistry (10), © Religious Education, University of Strathclyde (15 ALL), © Historical Picture Archive/CORBIS (18), akg-images / Jean-Louis Nou (20 LEFT), © World Religions Photo Library / Alamy (20 RIGHT), © Marco Brivio / Alamy (23), © V&A Images (25), © James Sturcke / Alamy (28), © Ross McArthur / Alamy (32 LEFT), © Kamal Kishore/Reuters/Corbis (32 CENTRE), © Around the World in a Viewfinder / Alamy (32 RIGHT), World Religions Photo Library/Chantal Boulanger (33), © David Samuel Robbins/CORBIS (36), PA/EMPICS (38 TOP), YUI MOK/PA/EMPICS (38 MIDDLE), Photolibrary.com (38 BOTTOM), superstock (39 TOP), © ACE STOCK LIMITED / Alamy (39 BOTTOM), Mary Evans Picture Library (41), Mari Darr-Welch / AP / EMPICS (42 LEFT), © Pablo Corral Vega/CORBIS (42 RIGHT), © Marc Garanger/CORBIS (43 LEFT), © BASSOULS SOPHIE/CORBIS SYGMA (43 RIGHT), Arvind Garg/CORBIS (45 TOP), © Religious Education, University of Strathclyde (45 BOTTOM), © GRAHAM TIM/CORBIS SYGMA (47), Z. Radovan / www.BibleLandPictures.com (52), © Larry Kolvoord/The Image Works/topfoto.co.uk (54), P.TOMKINS/VisitScotland/SCOTTISH VIEWPOINT (55), John Stillwell/PA/ EMPICS (64), © GYORI ANTOINE/CORBIS SYGMA (66), © BAZUKI MUHAMMAD/Reuters/Corbis (69), Mary Evans Picture Library (73), © Bettmann/CORBIS (77), Tzedek logo (81), © Edward Parker / Alamy (82), © Network Photographers / Alamy (84 TOP), FIONA HANSON/PA/EMPICS (84 BOTTOM), © Photofusion Picture Library / Alamy (85 TOP), © Tim Mosenfelder/Corbis (85 BOTTOM), TopFoto.co.uk (90), World Religions Photo Library (91), KocherPets, Inc. (92 TOP), © Randy Faris/CORBIS (92 LEFT LEFT), © Tiziana and Gianni Baldizzone/CORBIS (92 LEFT RIGHT), Israel's stamps are reproduced here by permission of the Israel Postal Authority (92 RIGHT BOTH).

Acknowledgements 'Ash Immersion', reproduced with permission of www.parmarth.com (29); 'As religious leaders strive to make sense of disaster, Archbishop of Centerbury admits there are no simple answers: "Where is God in all this?" – the problem for religions', Copyright Guardian Newspapers Limited 2005 (71); 'The Mother and Daughter', Copyright Guardian Newspapers Limited 2005 (77).
Every effort has been made to trace all copyright holders, but if any have been inadvertently overlooked the Publishers will be pleased to make the necessary arrangements at the first opportunity.

Although every effort has been made to ensure that website addresses are correct at time of going to press, Hodder Gibson cannot be held responsible for the content of any website mentioned in this book. It is sometimes possible to find a relocated web page by typing in the address of the home page for a website in the URL window of your browser.

Orders: please contact Bookpoint Ltd, 130 Milton Park, Abingdon, Oxon OX14 4SB. Telephone: (44) 01235 827720. Fax: (44) 01235 400454. Lines are open from 9.00 – 6.00, Monday to Saturday, with a 24-hour message answering service. Visit our website at www.hoddereducation.co.uk. Hodder Gibson can be contacted direct on: Tel: 0141 848 1609; Fax: 0141 889 6315; email: hoddergibson@hodder.co.uk

© Robert McVeigh and Joe Walker 2006
First published in 2006 by
Hodder Gibson, a member of the Hodder Headline Group
2a Christie Street
Paisley PA1 1NB

Impression number 10 9 8 7 6 5 4 3 2 1
Year   2010 2009 2008 2007 2006

Typeset in 12 on 14pt Giovanni by
Phoenix Photosetting, Chatham, Kent
Printed and bound in Italy.

A catalogue record for this title is available from the British Library

ISBN-10: 0 340-88988-8
ISBN-13: 978-0-340-88988-6

Contents

Teacher's Notes

Personal Search

This series of books is aimed at P7–S2 pupils. The authors believe that 'personal search' lies at the heart of religious and moral education (RME) and is 'a process by which pupils can discover and develop their own beliefs and values.' (*Effective Teaching of Religious and Moral Education: Personal Search*, LT Scotland 2001) This definition is in keeping with the National Guidelines: Religious and Moral Education 5–14 which state that one of the aims of RME is for pupils to 'to develop their own beliefs, attitudes, moral values and practices through a process of personal search, discovery and critical evaluation.'

The study of religions

The authors believe that RME is essentially about the study of religions and this study has a significant role to play in personal search in developing pupils' beliefs and values. Although a pupil's beliefs and values develop in a number of ways both within and outside school, the study of religions provides a distinctive approach.

It is helpful to study religion through its central features. The National Guidelines identify five key features – celebrations, festivals, ceremonies and customs; sacred writings, stories and key figures; beliefs; sacred places, worship and symbols (practices); and moral values and attitudes. In these Personal Search books each religion is explored through units relating to these key features as set out below.

Each book covers two religions. Religions have been paired according to their dates of origins: Hinduism and Judaism are the earliest, then Buddhism and Christianity, and finally Islam and Sikhism.

Although there is no explicit study of non-religious systems of belief such as Humanism, there are opportunities to consider non-religious stances for living, as well as religious stances, on issues such as the

	Festivals and celebrations	Stories and key figures	Beliefs	Practices	Values
Buddhism	Ordination	The Buddha's teaching	Impermanence	Meditation	Karuna
Christianity	Easter	The Sermon on the Mount	Creation	Holy Communion	Agape
Hinduism	Samskaras	The Ramayana	Reincarnation	Puja	Dharma
Judaism	Yom Kippur	The story of Esther	Suffering	Kashrut	Tzedakah
Islam	Ramadan	Muhammad	Submission	Hajj	Ummah
Sikhism	The Khalsa	Guru Granth Sahib	Mool Mantra	The Langar	Vand Chhakna

origins of the universe, the existence of God, suffering and evil, relationships and moral values.

Stimulus material

Each unit contains stimulus material for pupils to engage with. This includes texts, stories, creedal statements, personal testimonies and experiences. The aim of the stimulus material is to involve pupils in dialogue with religions so that they can find out about the beliefs and values of religious believers in an atmosphere of enquiry, openness and critical discussion.

Teaching and learning

Each unit begins with a statement of the content to be covered and identifies the main concepts and themes. Personal search questions and activities focus on these concepts and themes. The units make use of a process to enhance personal search which was first introduced in *Effective Teaching of Religious and Moral Education: Personal Search* (LT Scotland 2001). This process has **three** stages:

- Finding out
- Making connections
- Thinking it over

Finding out
This involves finding out about the beliefs, values and practices of religious traditions. Pupils should be encouraged to appreciate the importance of knowledge and evidence as the basis for developing their own beliefs and values, and for justifying their own opinions.

Making connections
This involves connecting other people's beliefs, values and practices to pupils' own ideas and life experiences. Pupils' experiences of family, friendships and belonging to a community already shape their intellectual,

social and moral development. This stage provides opportunities for pupils to reflect, talk about and share their own ideas and experiences.

Thinking it over
This involves creating opportunities for dialogue around the concepts and themes that emerge from the study of religions and pupils' own experience of life. Thinking it over should be challenging, dealing with issues that push children's thinking beyond the immediate knowledge of the content. The issues will invite discussion on a range of questions to do with God, suffering, evil, right and wrong, life and death, relationships, moral and social values, and the nature and origins of the natural world.

The three stages of the process need not take place in the order in which they are set out above. A unit may begin by finding out more about a religion, or perhaps by connecting with some aspect of pupil experience, or even by raising an issue for discussion. It is likely that discussion and activities will move backwards and forwards between each stage of the process.

Activities
Within the 'finding out' activities there are opportunities for further investigation and research. Pupils will need access to other resources including books, audio-visual materials and the Internet. In some of the 'making connections' and 'thinking it over' questions and activities teachers might encourage pupils to work together in small groups to discuss, share ideas and exchange views.

Choosing religions and units

There is no prescribed order in which religions or units within a religion should be studied. Schools might study one or more religions or select units from across religions using the key features.

Progression

The three books in this series provide materials for pupils throughout P7–S2. Pupils' maturity of thinking will develop over the three years, as will their reading, writing and interpretation skills. The units vary in terms of language level and difficulty of questions and tasks. Consequently, teachers should be selective with regard to these depending on pupils' age, stage and abilities. Attainment targets from the National Guidelines have not been included but teachers should use the Guidelines to ensure that pupils achieve their full potential.

Assessment

By looking at pupil responses to the various tasks, talking to individual pupils about their responses, and listening to pupils' discussion, teachers will be able to gather evidence about pupils' personal search skills. Pupils, through completing the activities in the books, should be able to state their views clearly on issues associated with the concepts identified at the beginning of each unit. They should be able to support these views with reasons and evidence in writing or in speech, and at some length. If pupils do this, they are demonstrating personal search skills.

Hinduism

Samskaras

In Hinduism there are a number of ceremonies that mark different stages in life. They begin before birth and end with death. These ceremonies are called samskaras. This unit will focus on some of the samskaras which take place at birth, during infancy and in later childhood. One of the important ceremonies is the Sacred Thread Ceremony. This ceremony marks the time when some young boys begin their study of Hindu teachings.

IN THIS UNIT YOU
WILL BE ASKED
TO THINK ABOUT:

✓ FAMILY

✓ STAGES IN LIFE

✓ THE FUTURE

✓ RESPECT

✓ IDENTITY

stimulus 1 Personal experiences

A number of people, of different ages and backgrounds, were asked to talk about a time in their life which meant a lot to them.

I could choose lots of things – the time we went on holiday to Florida was great and we had so much fun at Disneyland. It was just great being on such an exciting holiday with my family. I'll never forget the time I swam in a swimming competition and won. But I suppose the thing I remember most is my first day at Secondary School. I was so nervous. I knew I would be OK but I was still worried. It was a good job I could go with a couple of friends – that helped a lot. I've been at the school nearly a year now and it's great – lots to do and lots of new friends. But I'll never forget that first day – it's seems amazing now I was so nervous and worried.

Asha (age 12)

The best day of my life was when I got my Standard Grade Exam results. I reckon I could have worked a bit harder than I did. My mum was always nagging me – she said I'd probably regret not having worked harder. So I was a bit worried about the results. It took ages for the post to arrive that morning. I'd decided to take the envelope upstairs to be by myself but when it arrived, I just tore it open – 4 1s, 2 2s and 2 3s. Fantastic. My mum gave me a great big hug – I think she was more relieved than I was. I'll be doing Highers now. Then it was onto the mobile to find out how my mates had done. What a great day.

Oliver (age 16)

A time I will never forget happened last year. I was present in the hospital when my twin girls were born. It was the most wonderful experience of my life. When my wife started having labour pains, we drove to the hospital and then it happened so quickly. There they were, two small bundles of joy. I have to say I was very close to tears. It was really emotional. I felt really close to my wife. I was so pleased and so grateful. I'm not a religious person but I wanted to say a prayer of thanks. At the same time I also had a feeling of great responsibility. We were to be responsible for bringing up these two girls. Then the family came round – lots of flowers and presents. It was the greatest day of my life. I'll never forget it.

Peter (age 24)

At my age you spend a lot of time thinking about the past. I think I a lot about Jim, my husband, who died a couple of years ago. I think back about our life together. It wasn't always easy. We had our ups and downs, but I do so miss him, even now after two years. Sometimes I get my old photograph albums out when my son comes to visit me and we have a good talk about them. We have a laugh at my wedding photographs which seem so old fashioned now. Our wedding was so different from those today. I went to my great granddaughter's last year – well, the wedding and the reception. I said I couldn't face the disco at night – too noisy for me. My wedding seems like only yesterday – a nice church service and then a meal in a hotel for just family and a few friends – and then back to my husband's parents' house where we were going to live. I'll never forget that day. Nor will I forget the day he died. It was so sudden. We'd only been saying the day before he died how lucky we'd been – we'd hardly had a day's illness between us. But the very next day we got up and he collapsed and that was it. I didn't even have time to say goodbye to him – and that makes me very sad. We went back to the church we were married in for the funeral and that helped. I spend a lot of time thinking about him – good times and sad times.

Brenda (age 88)

FINDING OUT

❶ Look at the following list of words describing feelings. Match a feeling to a person and explain why you have made your choice:

joy, relief, nervousness, sadness

❷ Each of the accounts identifies turning points in that person's life. For each person identify these turning points.

❸ Explain how families are important in each of the accounts.

❹ What is a family? What different kinds of families are there?

❺ What is an 'extended' family? Find out how important the extended family is in Hinduism.

MAKING CONNECTIONS

❶ Talk about each of the reflections, and share experiences of similar events you know about.

❷ Write down your own account of a time in your life which was important to you. Describe your feelings at that time.

❸ Do a drawing with a heading to illustrate your account and contribute to a wall display of personal accounts.

❹ In what ways has your family influenced you in your life so far? How do you feel about that?

❺ What contribution do you feel you make to family life? Do you think your contribution is appreciated? Why do you say that?

❻ What have you learned from your family
a. about yourself and
b. about life in general?

Thinking it over

1 What would you say are the most important factors that contribute to a stable family life? Is stable family life sometimes difficult to achieve? What factors outside the family can make it more difficult?

2 Do you think families have a strong influence or a weak influence on young people's behaviour and beliefs? Why or why not? What other factors can influence a young person's behaviour and beliefs? Do these sometimes come into conflict with the family's influence? What can happen?

3 Do you think stable families are important for a stable society? Why or why not?

4 Do you agree or disagree that families were more important in the past than they are now? Give reasons for your answer.

stimulus
2 ***The journey through life***

The stimulus below identifies 16 samskaras.

1. Conception
2. Early pregnancy (2–3 months)
3. Later pregnancy (5–8 months)
4. Day of birth
5. Day of naming (10–12 days)
6. First outing (3–4 months)
7. Eating first solid food (6 months)
8. First haircut (Boys only 1–3 years)
9. Piercing the ear (3–5 years)
10. Sacred Thread Ceremony
11. Starting to learn the Hindu Scriptures
12. End of education
13. Marriage
14. Householder rituals and looking after a family
15. Retirement
16. Death and cremation

The Importance of Samskaras

Samskaras have been part of our way of life for thousands of years and details about them are found in our Holy Books. For us Hindus life is a sacred journey and samskaras are the way we mark important moments in our journey through life. They begin with our conception before birth and the last is when we die. Part of my job as a priest is to help people mark these important moments. I often lead the ceremony and say the prayers and chant the mantras from our Holy Books asking God to bless and protect the person at that important time in their life. Such occasions are usually very happy occasions, and it is good to share these times with family and friends.
(A Hindu Priest)

Hindu priest

FINDING OUT

❶ Identify the samskaras which are connected with
  • pre-birth
  • babyhood and childhood
  • being a student
  • adulthood.

❷ Some of the samskaras have approximate ages next to them. Some do not. Why do you think this is?

❸ Explain in your own words the main purpose of samskaras.

❹ What part does a Hindu priest play in samskaras?

❺ Samskaras mark important stages in the life as a Hindu journeys through life. Design a diagram which shows this. For example, your diagram could include a ladder or steps.

❻ Why do you think Hindus describe life as a 'journey'?

MAKING CONNECTIONS

❶ Draw a flow chart of your life so far and mark on it the important stages and turning points in your life.

❷ Look again at each of the personal reflections in Stimulus 1. Describe events that could have been marked by a special ceremony or ritual.

❸ Have you enjoyed your own 'journey' through life so far? What has been the best part?

❹ What might be your next big stage in life? How might you mark it? Are you looking forward to it? Why or why not? Do you see it as a turning point? In what way?

❺ In groups collect pictures of people from magazines. Sort them into sets according to what age or stage of life they are at. Discuss how you made your decisions.

Thinking it over

❶ Do you like your present age? Would you like to be older, or younger, or are you happy at your present age? Why?

❷ Do you agree with Hinduism that there are different stages in life from birth to death? What would you say they are? Why do you think they are called 'stages'?

❸ Can people of different ages understand each other? What can sometimes make it difficult? Is it important for people of different ages and stages in life to understand each other? Why or why not?

❹ 'Today is the first day of the rest of your life'. How far do you think we can plan our whole life? Should we try to? What would we need to take into account when making any such plan?

stimulus 3 Samskaras at birth and infancy

Here are some extracts from the diary of a Hindu mother describing samskaras of her son at birth and in infancy.

4 March 2003

Great day. Tiring day. Baby born at last. A son. After the baby was carefully washed, Rajaat (husband) placed honey on the baby's tongue. Honey is sweet and we are hoping the baby has a sweet life and a sweet nature. Rajaat then traced the 'Aum symbol' onto the baby's tongue. We then said some prayers together for the baby.

Aum symbol

The aum symbol is chanted by Hindus. It is believed by Hindus to be a sacred sound as it was the first sound ever heard. It represents God.

Two Hindu Prayers for a baby

Oh dear child, I give you this honey that has been provided by God who is the producer of all the wealth in the world. May you be preserved and protected by God and live in this world for 100 autumns.

O child, may you become firm and strong like a rod. May you become an axe to destroy injustice, may you become bright as gold with knowledge and action.

Here are some popular Hindu names and their meanings.

Boys   Padreep . . . . . Light
           Rajaat . . . . Courage
           Sanjay . . . . . . Victorious

Girls   Anjali . . . . Tribute
           Asha . . . . Expectation
           Meena . . . . . . Precious Stone

You can find out more about names at www.hindunet.com

13 March 2003
Baby 10 days old today. The priest came to lead our naming ceremony. He had prepared a horoscope for our baby. He'll use it later in life when he decides to get married to choose a good day to get married on. We've decided to call the baby Pradeep which means Light. Lots of our family and friends came. We'd got new clothes for the baby and we put Pradeep into a swinging cot and surrounded it with diva lamps. It was all very peaceful. The lamps made the room feel warm, and we are hoping our baby will feel warm and secure for the rest of his life. The priest announced the baby's name and then said prayers. It was a great celebration, and we gave Pradeep a special present of jewellery.

3 July 2003
Another milestone. Pradeep is 4 months old tomorrow and it is time for him to go outside to meet the big wide world. In the morning we'll take him out to see the sun and feel its warmth. Then we'll go to the temple. We hope that he will be a regular worshipper at the temple when he grows older.. The priest will bless him and show him the images of our gods, and pray for his health and happiness. Later that day, when night falls, we'll show him the moon.

4 September 2003
It's unbelievable. Pradeep is 6 months old. Time flies. He's now ready to have more than just milk. He's really growing up. We decided to give him some cooked rice, and yoghurt.

6 July 2004

Pradeep has a fine head of hair. He's now just over 16 months old. We've decided to give him his first haircut tomorrow. We do this because we believe in reincarnation. That means he has had previous lives, and so shaving his head of hair is a sign of removing all the badness from his previous life. I don't expect he'll enjoy having it done but we'll have something ready to cool his head afterwards.

FINDING OUT

❶ From the list of samskaras in Stimulus 2 identify those that are described in the diary entries.

❷ Draw a timeline for a male Hindu baby's first few years of life, marking on the samskaras.

❸ What is Aum?

❹ Honey is given to the child at birth to signify the hope that the baby will have a sweet life and a sweet nature. What do you think is meant by a sweet life and a sweet nature?

❺ What hopes for the baby are being described in the prayers?

❻ Explain why the first haircut is marked by a samskara.

❼ What is the purpose of preparing a horoscope for the baby?

Thinking it over

❶ Horoscopes play a big part in the lives of Hindus. What are your views about horoscopes? Do you believe they tell the future? Why do you think horoscopes are so popular?

❷ If it were possible to know the future would you want to? Why or why not? Do you think we can sometimes tell if we are going to have good or bad luck?

❸ Are there some things in life that are always a matter of luck? To what extent do we make our own luck?

❹ What is meant by the phrase 'What will be will be'. Do you agree or disagree with that way of looking at life?

❺ What benefits, if any, do you think there are for a Hindu family in performing the 'early years' samskaras?

stimulus **4**

Upanayana: The Sacred Thread Ceremony

Sometime after the age of eight some Hindu boys undergo the Sacred Thread Ceremony. Hindu boys begin what Hindus call the student stage of life, when they begin to learn more about the various rules and rituals of Hinduism. It is an important turning point in their life. An important part of the student stage is the relationship between the student and his teacher.

A Hindu student and his teacher

The Sacred Thread Ceremony traditionally took place when a boy left home to live with his teacher. Today the ceremony is often held in the home. Not all Hindu boys undergo this ceremony. It is only for those who belong to certain caste groups. At the ceremony the boy has a thread tied on him which has been blessed by a priest. The thread is made up of three strands of cotton. Each strand represents a debt and a duty.

> A boy has a debt to God – so he should worship God
> A boy has a debt to his parents – so he should love and respect his parents
> A boy has a debt to his teacher – so he should listen to his teacher.

The Sacred Thread Ceremony marks the beginning of a boy's religious responsibilities. From now on he is ready to study the Hindu scriptures and carry out worship at the family shrine. When he becomes a man, he will have the responsibility of making sure his family carries out its religious duties. Prayers will be said at the ceremony, including one known as the Gayatri Mantra which has been described as one of the main prayers of Hindus. Upanayana, the name of the ceremony, means 'Getting closer to God'.

The Gayatri Mantra

O God! You are the giver of life,
The healer of pains and sorrows
The giver of happiness

O Creator of the Universe
Send us your purifying light
And lead our thoughts in your ways.

Ancient Hindu teaching about what is expected of a student

He shall obey his teacher.
He shall do what is serviceable to his teacher, he shall not contradict him.
He shall always occupy a couch or seat lower than that of his teacher.
He shall not sleep in the daytime.

Let him not be addicted to gossiping.
Let him be discreet.
Let him be forgiving.
Let him be modest.
Let him be energetic.
Let him be free from anger.
Let him be free from envy.

A prayer which might be said together by a teacher and a pupil

May God protect us both
The teacher and the follower
May he feed us both
May we work together with energy
May our studies be vigorous and fruitful
May there be love and harmony between us.

Important Values

The Sacred Thread Ceremony marks the beginning of studies. The boy is leaving childhood behind and preparing for manhood. The boy must demonstrate important values, especially self discipline, concentration in studies, and respect for his elders and teachers.

❶ Share experiences of other initiation ceremonies you know about.

❷ How do the rules contained in the Hindu teaching about the behaviour of a student compare with the rules in your own class and school?

❸ Read the Hindu teaching about student behaviour. Think about what makes a good teacher. Write a poem (in the form of a list) about an ideal teacher beginning 'Let the teacher...'

❶ The sacred thread is made up of three strands of cotton. What do they represent?

❷ Explain how the boy might be said to have three debts?

❸ Copy and complete the chart below

Debt	Duty
To God	
	Love and respect
To teacher	

❹ According to Hindu teaching what qualities is a student expected to have?

❺ Look at the Gayatri Mantra. What is a mantra? What does this mantra teach about Hindu belief in God?

❻ Why is the Sacred Thread Ceremony regarded as an 'initiation' ceremony?

Thinking it over

❶ One of the important values a Hindu student has to demonstrate is respect. What does it mean to show respect for someone? Can you respect someone you don't like? Is it ever right not to show respect to someone? Can you give an example?

❷ 'Of all the turning points in life, the change from childhood to adulthood is the most important and difficult.' Do you agree or disagree? Give reasons for your answer. Would having a special ceremony at this time help? Why or why not?

❸ What do you think makes a person grown up? What kind of things do young people do to try and prove they are grown up? What do you think of some of these? Do you think that children today want to grow up too quickly? What makes you say that?

The Ramayana

This unit involves the study of a famous Hindu story, the Ramayana. It tells the story of how Rama is banished from his home for 14 years together with his wife Sita. While living in the depths of the forest Sita is kidnapped by the demon king, Ravana. The story goes on to tell how Sita is rescued by Rama with the help of the monkey king, Hanuman. The unit introduces an important Hindu concept – avatar – the belief that God descends to earth in animal or human form, from time to time, to save the world.

IN THIS UNIT YOU WILL BE ASKED TO THINK ABOUT:

✓ HEROES AND HEROINES
✓ GOOD AND EVIL
✓ ROLE MODELS
✓ WISDOM
✓ POWER

stimulus 1

Heroes and heroines

1. My hero is **Nelson Mandela.** I have chosen him because of what he did and the sort of person he is. He fought against apartheid in South Africa, fighting for the rights of all people, regardless of their colour or race, to have the right to vote. Because of this he spent many years in prison. Yet when he was freed he showed no bitterness against those who put him there. He became the first President of a South Africa where everybody had the vote whatever their colour, not just white people. People all over the world admire him.

A number of people were asked about their heroes and heroines. These are their responses.

2. When I was a young boy I read a book called *No Surrender*. This was the story of **Captain Scott** and his epic journey to the South Pole. He wanted to be the first person to reach the South Pole but another explorer beat him. On the way back from the Pole he and his companions had to endure dreadful conditions of cold and snowstorms. In the end the weather beat them. They were stuck in a tent with a raging blizzard outside. They could go no further and eventually they died in a tent not many miles from safety. This story of great courage has always inspired me and he is my hero.

4. My hero is just an ordinary person. She never meant to do anything special. **Lisa Potts** was a nursery nurse, working with young children. One day she was going about doing her job when a man with a machete entered the nursery. Without any thought for herself she helped get the children to safety but was attacked by the man, receiving lots of cuts. It took a long time for the damage to her arms to heal. Later she received the George Medal for her bravery. I think she is a hero because she put the children first before herself.

3. I have chosen as my hero a person called **Jane Tomlinson**. A few years ago Jane Tomlinson discovered she had cancer which the doctors said was terminal. Jane decided that she was going to get the most out of life and not let the cancer take charge of her life. Since that time she has done remarkable feats of endurance to raise money for charity. She has done marathons, cycling events, and triathlons. One of the hardest things she did was an ironman triathlon – 2 miles swimming, 112 miles cycling and a marathon. Often she is in a lot of pain doing these things. She has raised something like a million pounds for cancer and children's charities. Doing something for others, when life is tough for you, is something I really admire.

5. My hero lived in America in the 1950s. In some towns at that time, when travelling on buses, black people had to stand to let white people sit down if there was a shortage of seats. One day **Rosa Parks** was coming home from work and she was tired. She was told to stand up for a white person. She refused. She wouldn't budge. This started off the movement for getting black people in America equal rights. I admire her because she stood up for her rights.

❶ Read the stories relating to each of the five heroes and decide which of the following values they demonstrated. Each value may relate to more than one person. Copy the table below and tick the appropriate boxes.

❷ Which of the five people described above do you admire most? Why? What values did he or she demonstrate? Find out more about him or her and report back to the class.

❸ What are 'values'? Try to find a definition.

Values	Nelson Mandela	Captain Scott	Jane Tomlinson	Lisa Potts	Rosa Parks
Courage					
Standing up for what you believe					
Fighting for justice					
Concern for others					
Determination to succeed					

MAKING CONNECTIONS

❶ Who are your heroes and heroines? Write your own 'My hero is...' statement. If you are stuck for ideas look at the website www.myhero.com.

❷ Organise a survey amongst friends and family. In the survey find out who they admire as a hero, why they think that person is a hero, and what they think makes a hero. Contribute to a class book on the theme 'heroes'.

❸ What do you value most? Why do you say that?

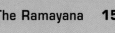

stimulus 2 *The Ramayana*

Characters

King Dasaratha	**Queen Kaikeyi**, the King's youngest wife
Rama, a prince, the King's son	and Rama's stepmother
Lakshmana, a prince, Rama's brother	**Bharata**, son of the Queen Kaikeyi
Sita, a princess	**Ravana**, the evil demon
	Hanuman, King of the monkeys

Prince Rama

Demon Ravana

Princess Sita

Hanuman, King of the monkeys

Rejoicing at the palace: Rama wins Sita as his bride

Today at last Sita has found a husband. Her father had said only someone who was worthy of her could marry her. So he set a task. If anybody could string a great bow, he would be allowed to marry his daughter. Many had come, all had failed. They couldn't even lift the bow. But today Prince Rama, son of King Dasaratha of Adoyha decided he would try. All came out to watch. He stepped up, took the bow in his hands and with a mighty effort he strung the bow. His strength was so great that he snapped the bow into pieces. How the crowd cheered. Sita's face was a picture. You could tell she was so pleased. Rama was obviously the prince she wanted to marry. Sita's father said 'This is the man worthy of my daughter. He is strong enough to protect her.' They hope to marry soon and live in Adoyha at Dasaratha's palace.

Tragedy in forest: Sita kidnapped by Ravana

News has just reached us of a terrible crime. Sita has been kidnapped by that most wicked of all villains, Ravana. We know from his past deeds that he is the most evil of all beings. Seemingly he had been stalking her for some time. His plan was so cunning. By his magical powers he conjured up a beautiful golden deer. Sita was entranced by it, and asked Rama to capture it. Rama soon got lost in the forest looking for it and Lakshmana went off to find him. Before going he drew a circle around their hut and told Sita that if she did not cross the line she would be safe. Ravana turned himself into an old man and approached the hut. He asked Sita for food. Sita was full of compassion for this hungry looking old man, and crossed the line. Immediately Ravana scooped her up with his twenty arms and carried her off in his flying chariot, taking her across the sea to his castle on the island of Lanka. We fear for her safety.

Crisis at the palace: Rama sent into exile

There has been a great row at the royal palace about who will be the next king when Dasaratha dies. It was widely thought that he had promised the throne to Rama. However late last night it was revealed that his wife, Queen Kaikeyi has persuaded him to make her son, Prince Bharata, the next king. Many years ago she had saved the King's life, and now she was asking to be rewarded. Palace officials say the King was not very happy about this but he felt he must keep his promise. To make matters worse, the Queen has said that there will be trouble if Rama stays, and so he has been sent into exile. Rama told his father that he should not worry about it because it was his duty as a loyal son to obey his father and he would go the very next day. Even at this moment Rama and Sita are packing. They leave in the morning, with Rama's brother Lakshmana. They cannot return for 14 years. The palace is in turmoil.

Battle in Lanka: Ravana killed, many casualties

With the help of Hanuman, the Monkey King, Sita has been rescued. The first problem Rama, Lakshmana and Hanuman faced was how to get across the sea. There was no bridge. They had no boat. They couldn't fly like Ravana. Hanuman had an idea. He called his monkeys together and they collected stones. Using magic, Rama made the stones float and they built a floating bridge across the water to Lanka. On land, there was a terrible battle. Ravana had a massive army. Rama's army was small. In the end it came down to single combat between Rama and Ravana. Ravana seemed indestructible. Every time Rama cut off one of his heads another grew in its place. But eventually, using a special weapon from the God Brahma, Rama aimed it at the heart of Ravana and he fell dead. The world has been saved from the greatest evil it has ever known.

Sita proves herself

There has been a surprise development in the great story of Rama and Sita. After the battle, when everybody was recovering, there was another crisis. Sita had spent many months as a prisoner with Ravana – a woman alone with wickedness. She had refused to marry him, but was she still pure? Her honour had been compromised. How could she prove she was pure? Sita ordered a fire to be built and then lit. She threw herself on the fire and amazingly Agni, the God of fire, rose out of the flames and handed back Sita out of the flames. She had undergone this test of fire, and proved to everyone that she was pure.

Rama and Sita return home: great rejoicing

Rama, Sita and Lakshmana have returned home. They arrived late last night when it was dark and the people put out diwa lamps to show them the way. Prince Bharata greeted them warmly, saying that Rama should be the king. We are sure he will turn out to be the best king and wisest ruler we've ever had.

1 About the story:
  a. How did Rama prove that he was worthy of marrying Sita?
  b. Describe the circumstances that led up to Rama's and Sita's exile.
  c. How did the evil Ravana succeed in capturing Sita?
  d. Describe the events leading up to the death of Ravana.
  e. How did Sita prove she was still pure and had not been influenced by the evil Ravana?
Study the actions of each of the characters (Rama, Sita, Lakshmana and Hanuman) and say what values you think they showed. Use the following words to help you:

devotion, wisdom, courage, good, faithful, loyal, loving

2 In groups, take a different aspect of the story and produce a cartoon strip. Then join the different parts together to produce a wall chart of the whole story.

3 What other stories do you know in which good defeats evil? Draw up a class list.

Thinking it over

1 Brainstorm the words 'good' and 'evil'. What is a good action? What is an evil action? Is it always clear what is good and what is evil?

2 Do you think today's world is a good or an evil place? What evidence would you put forward to support your view?

3 What makes people good or evil? Are people born evil or does it depend on what happened to them when they were young?

4 Do you think most people are a mixture of good and evil? Is there some good in everybody, including the most evil people you can think of?

3 Why the Ramayana is so important for Hindus

Rama and Sita. For many Hindus it was more than watching a play on television, it was an act of worship.

The Ramayana An Immortal Tale

The ideal person

The story of the Ramayana represents, through Lord Rama, an obedient son, a grateful disciple, a generous brother, an ideal husband, a man of true promise, a dutiful king, a great warrior, a forbearing personality, and a perfect human being. He can never be forgotten by any Hindu, to whatever caste or creed he may belong.
(Nila Pancholi – *Six World Faiths*)

A well-known story

'Almost every individual living in India is aware of the story of the Ramayana. Everyone, whatever age, outlook, education knows the essential part of the epic and adores the main figures of Rama and Sita. Every child is told the story at bedtime.'
(R.K. Narayan – Introduction to the Penguin edition)

The Ramayana on TV

When a version of the Ramayana was serialised on television in India on Sunday mornings, millions were glued to their televisions. Life came to a standstill; the streets were empty while everybody watched the latest instalment in the adventure of

FINDING OUT

❶ On the book cover it says the Ramayana is an 'immortal tale'. What do you think this means?

❷ In what ways is the story:

   a. an adventure?
   b. about love?
   c. about wisdom?

❸ What evidence is there that the Ramayana is popular among Hindus? Why do you think this is?

❹ What do you think is meant by the claim that watching a television version of the Ramayana was, for some Hindus, an act of worship?

❺ Explain what is meant by the 'ideal' person and 'perfect' human being.

MAKING CONNECTIONS

❶ What do you think the ideal person would be like? Could you ever be like that?

❷ Do you have someone you look up to as a role model? Who is it? Why?

❸ Would you be a good role model for a younger person? Why or why not?

❹ Choose one of the qualities shown by Rama or Sita or Hanuman. Write about a time when you have shown that quality or have witnessed that quality in another person.

Thinking it over

❶ Who do you think would make the better role model, someone you know really well or a famous person? Give reasons for your answer.

❷ Is there or has there ever been an ideal person? Would an ideal person have to be perfect?

❸ What does it mean to be wise?

❹ Do you need to know a lot to be wise? What, if anything, do you need to know to be wise?

❺ Do you have to be old to be wise? What could help you to become wise?

❻ 'The Ramayana can teach us a lot about how to be a better person.' Do you agree or disagree? Why?

stimulus **4** *Festivals*

Name of festival	Dassehra	Diwali
Time of Celebration	September/October	October/November
What it celebrates	In some parts of India this festival is associated with the story of the exile of Rama, the kidnapping and rescue of Sita and the killing of Ravana.	This festival celebrates the return of Rama and Sita to their homeland of Ayodhya after the defeat of Ravana. They were greeted with diwa lamps to light their way home.
Celebration customs	A major part of the celebration is the building of an effigy of Ravana containing hay and crackers. A person dressed as Rama fires a flaming arrow at the effigy to set it alight. In villages the story of the Ramayana might be acted out.	People place diwa lamps inside their houses. They are also placed in extended rows outside the house and lit in the evenings.

Name of festival	Dassehra	Diwali
Time of Celebration	September/October	October/November
Meaning of celebration	The celebration is especially enjoyed by children and is a reminder that evil will always fail and goodness will always win.	The celebration focuses on the welcome home Rama and Sita were given, and reminds Hindus of the good qualities of Rama and Sita.

An effigy of Ravana

A diwa lamp

FINDING OUT

❶ What part of the Ramayana is remembered at Dassehra?

❷ What part of the Ramayana is remembered at Diwali?

❸ Explain how the customs at both Dassehra and Diwali help remind Hindus of the story of Rama and Sita.

❹ What do Hindus learn from the celebration of Dasshera and Diwali?

Stimulus 5: Avatar

One of the important ideas in Hinduism is 'avatar', which means the appearance or descent of a god. In Hinduism one of the main gods is Vishnu. His task is to use his great power to preserve and protect the world. In times of crisis, such as when there are great disasters or cruel tyrants, he appears on earth in the form of an animal or human to save the world. Rama is the seventh avatar of Vishnu and the story of his saving the world is told in the Ramayana. Other avatars include Krishna (the eighth avatar) and Siddhatta Gotama, The Buddha (the ninth avatar).

Whenever righteousness decays, and unrighteousness rises up, I put myself forth. I come into being in every age to rescue the good, destroy the evil doers, and establish righteousness.
(Bhagavad Gita, sacred Hindu writings)

FINDING OUT

❶ Explain the role of an 'avatar' within Hinduism.

❷ According to the teaching of the Bhagavad Gita, what three things does Vishnu come to do?

❸ What is 'righteousness'?

❹ Find out more about the god Vishnu and other avatars. The website www.hindunet.com will help you.

Thinking it over

❶ Do you think the world today needs saving? What particular dangers do you think the world faces?

❷ If a 'God' descended to earth today, what do you think is the first thing the 'God' should do? Why?

❸ In groups, choose one 'danger' facing the world and discuss what might be done to reduce it.

❹ If you had the power to 'do' anything you wanted, what would you do?

❺ What do people mean when they say 'Knowledge is power'?

❻ Why do you think it is that those who have power are often corrupted by it?

Reincarnation

What happens when we die? Is death the end or does life go on in some form? This unit explores Hindu beliefs about death and what happens after it, and looks at how funerals are carried out in India and in this country. It introduces a number of important concepts – atman, reincarnation, samsara, karma and moksha.

IN THIS UNIT YOU WILL BE ASKED TO THINK ABOUT:

✓ DEATH AND WHAT HAPPENS AFTER IT

✓ IDENTITY

✓ RIGHT AND WRONG

✓ REMEMBERING

stimulus 1 *Funeral ceremonies*

This letter describes a funeral in a village in India. It was written by a man to his sister who lives in Britain and was unable to attend the funeral.

Dear Kamala

Well the funeral is over. Dad has been cremated. Mother was disappointed that you were not able to attend, but she does understand that having a husband and two young children it was difficult to get away and make the long journey. We both know that you would have wanted to be with us at this time and that not being there was very sad for you.

Everything went according to plan. As the eldest male relative, I had to organise everything. First I had to get the doctor to sign the death paper and then I asked the priest if he would come and say prayers. On Wednesday night, together with our male cousins, we carefully washed Dad's body and dressed him in new clothes. He looked very peaceful. In a way it was good that the pain of his last illness was now over.

Thursday was the day of the cremation. Our village cremation ground is near our local river. We placed dad's body on a stretcher, covering it with a cloth and placing flowers on it. I walked in front of the body as the stretcher was carried by our cousins and my eldest son to the cremation ground. We built a funeral pyre of wood and placed dad's body on top of it, the feet facing south. Our priest then placed camphor and sandalwood onto the pyre and said prayers.

As you know, as the eldest son, it was my responsibility to light the fire. Whilst the priest was praying I lit the fire, placing ghee onto the fire to make sure it burnt well. As the fire burnt family and friends threw offerings of nuts and rice onto the fire. This was a quiet time. We all had our memories of dad, and in a way it was very comforting. We stayed and watched until it was clear that dad's body had completely burnt. We then washed in order to purify ourselves. On Saturday we'll return to collect the ashes. I'll be in touch with you to discuss what we should do with them.

Love Ajay

Hindu cremation

Hindu Funerals in Britain

Hindu funerals will be held at the nearest
crematorium. Before the body goes to the
crematorium, it is likely to be left in the
funeral parlour of an undertaker. The
undertaker will probably be responsible for
washing and dressing the deceased person.
Mourners will visit their deceased relative at
the funeral parlour. Customs at the funeral
parlour that might be carried out include
placing sandalwood or joss sticks around the
corpse and placing a garland of flowers
round the neck of the deceased person.
Relatives and friends might offer the dead
person a flower as a way of saying goodbye.
At the crematorium, the priest will read from
the Hindu scriptures. As the coffin departs,
the mourners will perhaps stand and chant
the name of Rama. Later, relatives will return
to collect the ashes.

A Hindu prayer often said at a funeral

O God
Like a ripe watermelon
This fruit was ready to be plucked
When the time is ripe for me
Please grant me liberation
As this has happened now.

❶ What duties did Ajay have to perform before the cremation ceremony?

❷ Describe how the cremation was carried out in India.

❸ How different is the cremation ceremony in Britain from what happened in India? What similarities are there?

❹ What do you think the Hindu prayer means?

Thinking it over

❶ It is very sad when someone dies. How do people normally show their sadness? What is mourning? Why do you think it is important?

❷ In what ways might a funeral help to comfort those who have been bereaved?

❸ Which version of the cremation ceremony, the Indian or the British, do you think would be more satisfying for relatives? Give reasons for your answer.

❹ A funeral can sometimes be a time of celebration as well as sadness. In what circumstances might a funeral reflect the idea of celebration?

❺ In Britain people who die are either cremated or buried. What ideas and beliefs do you think lie behind these quite different ceremonies?

stimulus 2 *Hindu beliefs*

Sanjay discusses with Julie what Hindus believe about death and what happens after it.

Julie: Sanjay, can you tell me something about what Hindus believe happens when you die?

Sanjay: Well, we believe every living being, humans and all creatures, contains a force of life and energy. We call this atman. Sometimes people use words like soul or spirit or divine energy to describe it. We believe that when any living creature dies, his or her body dies, but their atman lives on and remains the same.

Julie: So when a person's body dies, what happens to their atman?

Sanjay: We believe that when our body dies, our atman is released from the body and enters another body. I'm sure you know that this belief is called reincarnation. 'Re' means again and 'incarnation' means being born into a body.

Julie: So this is very different from people who believe that a person is born, lives their life, dies and then there is some sort of life after death. For you life is continuous. You are born, live, die and then are born again, and this keeps on going.

Sanjay: That's right. We believe there is a cycle of life – birth, life, death, rebirth, life, death and so on. We call this cycle samsara. It's a bit like nature. In spring there is a sort of birth of new life which blooms in the summer. Then in autumn through into winter there is dying and death, and then it starts again with new life in spring.

Julie: One thing puzzles me. When people die and their atman gets a new body – how is it decided what body their atman enters?

Sanjay: Well, the body a person's atman enters depends on how well that person has lived their life. If they have lived a good life and their thoughts, words and actions have been good, then next time they will have a better life. If their life has been bad and their thoughts, words and actions bad, then next time they will have a worse life or even return as an animal or insect. The name we give to this belief is karma. Good actions have a good outcome whilst bad actions have a bad outcome.

Julie: So there's a good reason for trying to live a good life and do good actions.

Sanjay: That's right, how you live one life decides whether in the next life you come back higher or lower in the scale of existence.

Julie: I think I understand your beliefs a lot better now. Just one more thing – this cycle of life – it seems endless. It goes on and on. Is there ever an end to it?

Sanjay: Well, this is perhaps the hardest part to explain. As Hindus we believe that our ultimate goal in life is to escape from the cycle of birth, death and rebirth. To escape from samsara is to achieve moksha – a state of perfection and freedom from all earthly worries.

stimulus **3**   *Karma*

❶ In pairs or small groups, discuss the meaning of the following Hindu concepts – atman, reincarnation, samsara and karma. One person should record any questions that arise out of the discussions.

❷ Write the title 'Hindu beliefs'. Underneath write a definition of each of the concepts that you discussed and show how they all fit together to explain what Hindus believe happens after they die.

❸ Sanjay said that the idea of moksha was the most difficult to explain. Carry out research to find out more about what Hindus mean by moksha.

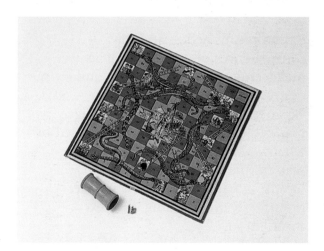

Moksha Patamu boardgame

Moksha Patamu is an ancient Indian game and the origin of snakes and ladders. It is a game of morality with the base of the ladder being located on squares representing forms of goodness and the snakes coming from squares representing various forms of evil. The game was used to teach children about the Hindu belief in karma. In the game landing on the good squares allows a player to ascend higher up the league of life, whereas landing on the evil squares sends a player back to the lower tiers of life. In the original game the squares of goodness included Faith, Reliability, Generosity and Knowledge. The squares of evil included Vanity, Vulgarity, Theft, Lying, Drunkenness, Debt, Rage, Greed, Pride, Murder and Lust.

> Actions which spring from the mind, from speech and from the body produce either good or evil results; by actions are caused the conditions of men, the highest, the middle and the lowest.
> (Bhagavad Gita, sacred Hindu writings)

> Karma means action and the consequences of action. Every act we make, and even every thought and every desire we have, shape our future experiences. Our life is what we have made it. And we ourselves are shaped by what we have done. Not only do we reap in this life the good and evil we have sown; they also follow us after physical death, affecting our next incarnation.
> (Mary Pat Fisher – *Religions Today*)

FINDING OUT

❶ Moksha Patamu is described as a game of morality. What is morality?

❷ If you were making the game of Moksha Patamu relevant for today's world suggest:
   a. two virtues you would keep from the original game
   b. two evils in the original game you would not keep
   c. two new virtues for the new game
   d. two new evils for the new game.

❸ What circumstances might turn people from wanting to do good to doing evil?

❹ What do you think is meant by 'we reap in this life the good and evil we have sown'?

MAKING CONNECTIONS

❶ The good thing about belief in karma is that it makes you think about your actions and whether they are right or wrong. Do you think about the consequences of your actions? Can you give an example? Looking back did you make the right decision?

❷ Describe a situation involving your relationships with others – either in your family or with your friends – in which you intended to do the right thing but it didn't work out as you expected. What happened? Was it your fault, the fault of others or a combination of both? Or was it due to changing circumstances?

Thinking it over

❶ How did you come to know the difference between right and wrong?

❷ What makes one thing right and another thing wrong?

❸ 'What's right for one person may be wrong for another'. Is right and wrong simply a matter of individual preference?

❹ Are there things which are always right and things which are always wrong?

❺ How old do you think a person needs to be before they can tell the difference between right and wrong?

Sometimes a new body is needed after a short while because of illness or injury or sometimes after many years when the body is old, tired and worn out.

stimulus 4 *Reincarnation*

'You only live once' is a belief that most people in the western world would adhere to. However, Hindus disagree. Instead, this present life is one of several, possibly numerous, lives that we have lived and will live.

Imagine a car driver and a car. The car depends on the driver. It needs the driver to make it move. The driver can be compared to the atman or soul of a person and the car to our physical body. In the same way as the car depends on the driver, so our physical body depends on the soul. The soul is the life force of the body. Eventually a car will need replacing. Perhaps a car might get damaged in a crash and cannot be used again or it becomes so old, battered and worn out that it has to be replaced. Similarly from time to time, the atman needs a new body.

Atman

Weapons cannot cut it, fire cannot burn it, water cannot wet it, wind cannot dry it.
(Bhagavad Gita, sacred Hindu writings)

Reincarnation

As a man casts off his worn out clothes and takes on other new ones in their place
So does the embodied soul
Cast off his worn out bodies
And enters others new
(Bhagavad Gita, sacred Hindu writings)

① Explain to a partner the idea of a car and its driver to explain atman and reincarnation.

② What conclusion about atman can you draw from the quotation on page 28?

③ Explain the idea of reincarnation contained in the second quotation on page 28.

④ Collect some examples of people who claim to recall incidents from a past life.

⑤ What are the arguments for and against reincarnation?

Thinking it over

① Are human beings and other living creatures purely physical or do they possess, as Hindus believe, a soul or spirit (atman)? What do you think?

② Some people believe that there is life after death? Do you? Can you explain why?

③ If it were possible to live for ever would it be a good thing?

④ Can you have more than one life? What makes you think so?

⑤ If we do not have memories of a past life does this mean that reincarnation is not true?

⑥ If we do have memories of a past life does this prove reincarnation?

⑦ *Death is the end. That's it – there's nothing more.*

After death it's heaven or hell. It depends on how you have lived your life.

At death your soul or spirit lives on and returns in another body.

Which opinion comes nearest to your own view? Why? Survey and record the views of the class.

---

stimulus 5

What happens to the ashes?

Hindus prefer that the ashes of the dead are immersed in a river, especially a Holy River such as the River Ganges in India. They believe that this helps bring them closer to moksha. In fact Hindus, if possible, wish to die on the banks of the Ganges and many cremations take place on steps leading down to the River Ganges. Although Hindus have no grave to visit, each year they hold a ceremony to remember their dead relatives. The notice on the following page describes the services offered by Parmarth Niketan which is an ashram located in Rishikesh, a town on the banks of the River Ganges. An ashram is a spiritual community where people go to engage in spiritual practices. The Parmarth Niketan Ashram offers an ash immersion programme.

The River Ganges

Hindu scriptures say that to immerse the ashes of a loved one in the holy waters of Mother Ganga (River Ganges) is to help their spirit progress towards liberation.

It is therefore every family's deepest wish to perform this sacred rite for their loved ones. People travel from across the world to Rishikesh, Varanasi and other holy cities on the banks of Mother Ganga in order to immerse their loved one's ashes in Mother Ganga's holy waters.

We have started a divine 'Ash Immersion' programme at Parmarth Niketan. In this program pure traditional pious puja (worship) will be done for your loved one's remains at no charge. You will be assured that the sacred rites are performed on the banks of Mother Ganga according to ancient scriptures by trained priests.

The programme can take place in one of two ways:

1. You can come personally to Parmarth Niketan Ashram in Rishikesh where puja will be arranged according to your schedule. All boarding and lodging will be provided for you at the ashram.

2. If it is not possible for you to make the journey yourself or to send family members, you can send the ashes to us by post with a letter including the details of the deceased (name, date of death, place of prior residence, names of mourning family members). Puja will be conducted here for you and as an acknowledgement photos will be sent to you afterwards.

FINDING OUT

1 Why do Hindus prefer the ashes of their dead relatives to be immersed in the River Ganges?

2 Describe the services offered by the Parmarth Niketan Ashram to help Hindus with ash immersion.

3 Rishikesh is an important pilgrimage centre on the banks of the Ganges for Hindus. What is a pilgrimage centre? Look up www.rishikesh.org and identify some of the activities that go on at Rishikesh.

4 In Britain people sometimes say they would like their ashes scattered over a place which means a lot to them. Do you know any examples of this being done? Share these with the rest of the class.

Thinking it over

1 Memorial stones, 'In memoriam' notices in newspapers, visiting a grave and looking at a book of remembrance are all special ways of remembering members of the family who have died. Is it important to remember family members who have died? Is it always easy to remember them? Would it help to have, as Hindus do, a special day each year to remember them?

2 What is Remembrance Day? Do you think we should remember those people who have lost their lives in defence of their country? Why or why not? Can you think of other people we should remember in this kind of way?

3 Imagine you had lived a long life and you are looking back on it. How would you want to remember it? What would you want to be remembered for? Should this affect what you do now?

 **Dharma**

indus call their religion sanatana dharma which means 'the eternal way of life'. The word dharma refers to the duties and responsibilities a person has in life. However not all Hindus have the same dharma. A person's dharma depends very much on what stage they are at in life.

IN THIS UNIT YOU WILL BE ASKED TO THINK ABOUT:

✓ AIMS IN LIFE
✓ WAR AND PEACE
✓ DUTIES
✓ RESPONSIBILITIES

stimulus 1 *Aims in life*

What are your aims in life?

These are some of the answers given by a group of young people when they were asked this question.

❶ Look at the list of aims in life. In groups, discuss what might be involved in each one and arrange them in order of importance – from most important to least important. Justify your choice of the most important and the least important.

❷ Do you have any aims for your life? How many? Do your aims include any of the ones on the list? Which ones?

❸ Are there any aims in the list that in your opinion should not be part of a list of aims in life? What makes you say that?

❹ If you were only allowed one aim in life what would it be? What kind of considerations would influence your decision? What thoughts do you have about how you might achieve that aim?

stimulus 2 Hindu teaching on the aims of life

Hindu teaching identifies four main aims in life and indicates how the highest aim might be achieved. The aims are set out in order of importance, from least important to most important.

Aims	What it means
1. Kama	Enjoyment of the good things in life
2. Artha	Earning enough money for the necessities of life
3. Dharma	Fulfilling religious, moral and social duties
4. Moksha	Freedom from the cycle of life and union with Brahman.

Moksha is the highest aim in life (See the unit on Reincarnation). In Hindu sacred writings three ways or paths are identified which can be followed by Hindus to help achieve Moksha. Most Hindus will live a life which tries to involve all three paths.

Path	What it means
1. Jnana Yoga	A life of studying Hindu teachings and spending time in contemplation and meditation
2. Karma Yoga	A life of selfless actions, thinking about other people
3. Bhakti Yoga	A life of devotion and prayer to a chosen deity.

FINDING OUT

❶ Kama refers to the 'good things in life' and Artha to 'the necessities of life'. Make two lists, one which includes the 'good' things in life and the other the 'necessities' of life. What is the difference between the two lists?

❷ Look at the list of aims in Stimulus 1. Which of them do you think are reflected in the Hindu aims for life?

❸ Match each of the paths to moksha to one of the following words:

service   worship   knowledge

❹ Find out more about the paths and write a short note on each.

❺ What do you think is meant by 'fulfilling religious, moral and social duties' (Dharma)?

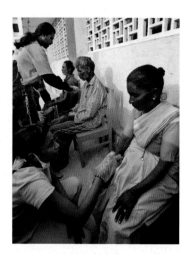

Jnana yoga, karma yoga, and bhakti yoga paths to obtain moksha

Thinking it over

❶ 'It's important to have an aim in life but many people have aims which they have no chance of fulfilling – they are too unrealistic.' Is it important that our aims are realistic? How can we make sure that they are realistic?

❷ What is meant by saying that sometimes we need to 'follow our dreams'? What is the difference between an aim and a dream? Can you give an example of someone who followed their dream and became successful? What do you think of people whose dream is to become 'famous'?

❸ Which aim in life do you think is the better one – to look after yourself or to look after others? Why? Can looking after yourself be described as selfish? Why or why not?

❹ Hinduism teaches that our aims in life must go beyond personal enjoyment and comfort to thinking about others and ultimately to thinking about our next life. How far do you agree with this?

❺ Do you think that having aims or purposes helps to give meaning to life? Is it better for a person to feel that their life has meaning than to feel that their life is meaningless? Why or why not?

❻ Do you think some people believe that they have no purpose in life at all? What kinds of circumstances might lead people to believe this?

stimulus 3 *Krishna and Arjuna*

This story about Krishna and Arjuna is found in the Bhagavad Gita, one of the most popular of the Hindu sacred writings. Arjuna is a prince, and Krishna a Hindu God who is acting as Arjuna's charioteer. Arjuna's dharma was to act as a prince and a soldier.

The story concerns a family at war with each other. One part of the family has cheated the other part out of some of its land. A battle is about to take place and Arjuna is fighting to retrieve the land that has been stolen from his side of the family.

Arjuna

There, Arjuna saw his uncles, grandfathers, teachers, maternal uncles, brothers, sons, grandsons, and comrades. Seeing fathers-in-law, all those kinsmen, and other dear ones standing in the ranks of the two armies, Arjuna was overcome with great compassion and sorrowfully said: O Krishna, seeing my kinsmen standing with a desire to fight, my limbs fail and my mouth becomes dry. My body quivers and my hairs stand on end. The bow, Gaandeeva, slips from my hand and my skin intensely burns. My head turns, I am unable to stand steady and, O Krishna, I see bad omens. I see no use of killing my kinsmen in battle.

…Having said this in the battlefield and casting aside his bow and arrow, Arjuna sat down on the seat of the chariot with his mind overwhelmed with sorrow.

(Bhagavad Gita 1.26–31; 1.47)

Krishna and Arjuna on the Chariot

As the time for the battle draws near, Arjuna begins to have second thoughts about the whole idea of waging war on his own family. He sees members of his family on the opposing side and knows he will have to kill some of them or be killed himself. Krishna argues with him. He reminds him of his duty. As a soldier and prince, Arjuna is expected to take up his weapons and fight. He must defend his family and their lands. To fulfil his dharma he must fight and get back what belongs to his family. In the end Krishna persuades him to go into battle and Arjuna is victorious.

Krishna

Considering also your duty as a warrior you should not waver. There is nothing more encouraging for a warrior than a righteous war. Only the fortunate warriors, O Arjuna, get such an opportunity for a war that is like an open door to heaven. If you will not fight this righteous war, then you will fail in your duty, lose your reputation, and incur sin. People will talk about your disgrace forever. To the honoured, dishonour is worse than death. The great warriors will think that you have retreated from the battle out of fear. Those who have greatly esteemed you will lose respect for you. Your enemies will speak many unmentionable words and scorn your ability. What could be more painful than this? You will go to heaven if killed, or you will enjoy the earth if victorious. Therefore, get up with a determination to fight, O Arjuna.

(Bhagavad Gita 2.31–8)

❶ Look at the picture of Krishna and Arjuna. Which is Krishna? Which is Arjuna? How can you tell?

❷ What was Arjuna so worried about?

❸ What do you think he meant when he said to Krishna, 'I see bad omens'?

❹ What do you think Krishna meant by referring to Arjuna's 'duty as a warrior'?

❺ What is a 'righteous war'?

❻ What arguments did Krishna use to persuade Arjuna to fight?

❼ Arjuna was faced with a dilemma. What is a dilemma? What was Arjuna's dilemma?

MAKING CONNECTIONS

❶ Every family has quarrels and disagreements. Can you remember being part of a family quarrel? What was it about? Who was to blame? How was it resolved?

❷ Collect together pictures or stories of recent wars and visit a local war memorial. What do they tell you about war?

❸ If possible talk to someone who has been involved in war about their experiences. Find out if they believed fighting was a duty.

❹ Think about a time when you faced a dilemma. What was the dilemma? How did you resolve it?

❺ What duties do you have as a son or daughter and as a student? How well do you think you carry these out? Can you give examples?

Thinking it over

❶ In groups, discuss what you think are the causes of war. Share your conclusions with the rest of the class.

❷ Can there ever be such a thing as a 'righteous' war? Give reasons for your answer.

❸ Winston Churchill is reputed to have said, 'Jaw jaw is better than war war.' What do you think he meant? Why do you think 'jaw jaw' doesn't always prevent war?

❹ Which of Krishna's arguments do you think would have been most effective in persuading Arjuna to fight? Do you think the argument would be just as effective today? Why or why not?

Gnhastha-ashrama – householder stage

The dharma of the householder stage of life can be summed up as taking care of the family, keeping the religious traditions alive in the family and being a good member of the community. According to Hindu sacred writings the householder stage is the most important stage of life because all the other stages depend on this one. The main duties are to:

- get married and have children
- care especially for the elderly members of the family who should be treated with great respect
- serve others by giving to charity and offering hospitality
- keep the customs and traditions of Hinduism, especially performing religious duties such as daily puja and the celebration of festivals.

stimulus 4 *Ashramas (stages in life)*

A person's dharma depends on his stage in life (ashrama). In Hinduism there are four stages in life. We looked at the first stage, the Student Stage, in the unit on samskaras. The other three are the Householder Stage, the Retirement Stage and the Renunciation Stage. Each of these stages has its own dharma. Going through all the stages is seen as the ideal pattern to a journey through life, but most Hindus do not go through all the stages in a lifetime.

> Having attended to his bodily calls… and having first washed the teeth, a twice-born man should offer the morning prayer. He should offer the food oblation. He should cast food in the ground for dogs, untouchables and crows.
>
> (Yajnavalkya Smriti Writings)

- a twice-born man is a man who has undergone the Sacred Thread Ceremony
- oblations are food offerings made during puja
- untouchables are Hindus who are outside the four main social groups.

Vanaprastha-ashrama – retirement stage

Vanaprastha-ashrama literally means the stage of a forest dweller. This was because in the past a man at this stage would have gone to live in the forest away from his family. Today he will stay with his family but may spend some time in an ashram in order to meditate and reflect. This stage may be summed up as giving less time and attention to the affairs of looking after a family, and thinking more about spiritual matters. The main duties are to:

- hand over family responsibilities to his eldest son
- spend more time in meditation, prayer and the study of sacred writings
- be available to give advice to younger members of the family because of his long and wide experience of the world.

Sannyasa – renunciation stage

Very few enter this stage of life. In this stage a man becomes a sadhu, a wanderer, possessing only a few things such as a staff (walking stick) and a begging bowl. This stage may be summed up as an attempt to get closer to the main aim in life (moksha): freedom from the cycle of life. The main duties are to:

- abandon the world and family life
- become a wandering hermit unhindered by family, home and possessions
- devote life to pilgrimage, meditation and studying the sacred writings.

> Rejoicing in the things of the spirit, caring for nothing, abstaining from sensual pleasure, himself his only keeper, he may live on in the world, in the hope of eternal bliss.
>
> (Vatsyayana writings)

> When a householder sees his skin wrinkled and his hair white and the sons of his sons, then he may resort to the forest.
>
> (Manu Smriti writings)

Sadhu

❶ What name do Hindus give to stages in life?

❷ What are the main duties of the householder stage?

❸ How does a Hindu in the retirement stage spend most of his time? What is an ashram?

❹ What is a sadhu? What does a Hindu in the renunciation stage do to try and achieve moksha?

❺ Design a poster headed with the four stages of life. Your poster should include the name and the duties of each stage.

MAKING CONNECTIONS

❶ What would you say were your main duties and responsibilities at your present stage of life? Do you think these will change as you get older? What events in particular might bring about changes?

❷ Is responsibility something you welcome? Why?

❸ Have you ever been given a responsibility you shouldn't have? Describe what happened. Who placed that responsibility on you? How did you feel about what happened?

Thinking it over

❶ The householder stage of life is regarded by Hindus as the most important. Why do you think this is?

❷ Look again at the duties and responsibilities of the renunciation stage. Why do you think sadhus are so admired and respected? In what ways might their lifestyle be considered selfish? Do you agree?

❸ What does it mean to be responsible for someone? Can you give an example?

❹ How old do you think young people need to be before they can be considered 'responsible adults'?

❺ What kind of things should people be allowed to do when they are 'responsible'? Are all adults responsible? Why do you think this is?

❻ What is the opposite of responsible? Can you give an example?

Puja

Puja is a form of Hindu worship. This unit focuses on how and why Hindus worship, both in the home and in the temple or mandir. It introduces some Hindu beliefs about Brahman and Shiva and explores some of the images that Hindus use to help them think about and worship God.

stimulus 1 ## *What is worship?*

IN THIS UNIT YOU WILL BE ASKED TO THINK ABOUT:

Personal Search

✓ YOUR OUTLOOK ON LIFE

✓ WHAT IS REAL AND NOT REAL

✓ CREATION

✓ PEACE OF MIND

Here are some definitions:

Worship (verb)

1. worship God or gods – venerate, pay homage to, praise, glorify, pray to, exalt
2. worship at the local church or temple – attend a service, pray, take part in religious rites
3. he worships his wife/the fans worship the film star – adore, be devoted to, cherish, idolise, hero-worship

Some people's lives can be dominated by the worship of one thing: a car or other special possession, a football team, a pop group, money, or even certain ideas.

I worship my football team. I never miss a match if I can help it.

I worship my car. I spend a lot of time cleaning and polishing it.

I worship a pop group. I have posters of them in my bedroom and all their CDs.

I worship my friends. I like to spend as much time as I can with them.

I worship money. I want to be a millionaire before I'm thirty.

Thinking it over

❶ Is there one thing in your life which takes up a lot of your time and energy or are there a number of things in which you are interested? Can you give examples?

❷ Do you think it is a good idea to have one thing in your life that dominates everything else? Why or why not?

❸ How do you think a situation like that comes about?

❹ Is it possible to change the thing or things that dominate your life? How easy or difficult do you think this would be? Would you want to?

❺ How would you describe your outlook on life – optimistic or pessimistic? What makes you say that?

FINDING OUT

❶ What different meanings are there of the word worship?

❷ Use a dictionary to find the meaning of the following words associated with worship: homage, adore, glorify, devotion, idolise.

❸ What are religious rites? Can you give an example from your studies in Hinduism?

❹ Working in groups, discuss the differences between the worship offered to God by religious believers, the worship given to a wife by her husband and the worship of a pop group by their adoring fans. Each group should record the main points of their discussion to share with the class.

❺ Devise a questionnaire to give to religious believers to find out how and where they worship and what they believe about God.

stimulus **2**

The focus of worship: Hindu beliefs about God

Hindus, at home and in temples, have images (statues) of different gods and goddesses. For RE homework Julie has to explain why Hindus have lots of images. She decides to ask Sanjay to help her.

Julie: Sanjay, I've got this RE homework – I've got to find out why Hindus have images of gods and goddesses. Can you help me? Do you believe in lots of gods?

Sanjay: Well it's true we have lots of images – we call them murtis. However it is not as simple as that. In fact, although we have lots of different gods and goddesses, we believe in one God. We call this God

Brahman. Brahman is said to be the one supreme spirit and power in the universe.

Julie: But if you believe in one God – why do you have lots of images of gods?

Sanjay: That's a bit easier to explain. Take my dad for example – he's a dad, a son, a brother, a husband. He's an accountant, he's a great singer, he's a part-time badminton player and so on. You're just the same – you have different roles in life, and you have different characteristics. You're great at Maths, useless at spelling. You're usually a calm placid person but sometimes you can fly off the handle. Because we cannot know Brahman completely we find it helpful to have many different ways of trying to understand Brahman and these are our gods and goddesses. There is a saying in one of our Holy Books 'God is one, but the wise call him by many names.' So each god and goddess tell us something about Brahman.

Julie: I think I understand why you have different gods and goddesses. Each of them helps you understand Brahman. But I'm not sure I understand why you have the images.

Sanjay: Well an image is visual, we can see it. Brahman has no form so we look at an image, and it tells us something about Brahman's character. Looking at an image helps us to think about an aspect of Brahman. So when we worship, we show devotion to our images, and this is our way of trying to get in touch Brahman.

Julie: Thanks Sanjay. I'd better get on with the homework. Perhaps a prayer to God would help?

Sanjay: Well, Hindus would pray to the goddess Sarawasti – because she is our goddess of learning.

A Hindu Prayer

You are mother, you are father
You are my friend, you are my teacher
You are my wisdom, you are my riches
O God you are everything to me
O God of all Gods.

FINDING OUT

❶ What name do Hindus give to the images of their gods and goddesses?

❷ Explain what Hindus mean when they say 'God is one, but the wise call him by many names.'

❸ Sanjay says that Brahman is 'the one supreme spirit and power in the universe'. What does this tell you about the importance of Brahman in Hinduism?

❹ What do you think is meant by 'Brahman has no form'? What does this tell you about Brahman?

❺ The prayer says, 'O God you are everything to me'. What does this tell you about Hindu belief in God?

❻ What name is given to the goddess of learning?

❼ Write your own answer to Julie's homework question. Include a sentence or two about the advantages for Hindus in having many different gods and goddesses to help them understand Brahman. Do you see any disadvantages in this practice?

MAKING CONNECTIONS

❶ What do we mean when we say we 'know' a person? What is it we know about them – their name, where they come from, their personality, their experiences, their secrets? Which of these aspects are easier and which are more difficult to learn about? Why?

❷ Do people sometimes hide their 'real' selves? What kind of things do people hide from others? Why? What do we mean when we talk about what people are like on the 'inside' as opposed to the

'outside'? What is the difference? Is the real person what is on the inside or what we see on the outside? Are we sometimes more interested in outward appearances?

❸ Can you think of a time when you thought you were looking at one thing and it turned out to be something else? Describe what you thought you saw and what it actually was.

❹ Look at examples of visual puzzles which reflect different images depending on how you look at it. Discuss whether you think there is one view which is real and one which is not.

A Gestalt puzzle. How many images can you see?

❺ We normally find out about our world through our senses. What are our most important senses? How do we use them to acquire information? Do you think we have a sixth sense? What do you think it is?

❻ If you can read some of the books which reflect the idea that there is another world beyond or parallel to the one in which we live: for example, The Narnia books by C. S. Lewis, The Harry Potter books by J. K. Rowling, and *His Dark Materials Trilogy* by Philip Pullman.

Thinking it over

❶ Many Hindus believe that only Brahman is real. The world we live in is an 'illusion'. What is an illusion? Do you think the world is real or an illusion?

❷ According to many Hindus the world exists but each of us only experiences it through our own senses, thoughts and memories. If we can only experience the world through our own senses, thoughts and memories, does this make it more or less likely that the world is real?

❸ Some people claim that there is more to the world, more to what is 'real', than we can see, hear and touch. They feel that the important thing is somehow hidden from us. Do you agree or disagree? Give reasons for your answer.

stimulus 3 *Looking at images of God*

Although there are many different images of God, most Hindus use only a few when at worship. One of the popular gods worshipped by Hindus is Shiva.

Case Study: The God Shiva

Shiva represents both destruction and creation. In the world today there are many examples of destruction. We see on news broadcasts the destructive power of nature, through storms, floods and avalanches. Destruction can also be the result of war and acts of terrorism. As individuals we also have moments when we can be destructive caused by feelings of hatred, jealousy and anger. Sometimes, however, creation can arise out of destruction. A tower block of flats in a city might be destroyed to make way for better housing. In nature a powerful hurricane destroys much in its path but it also results in a burst of new plant growth. An angry argument is hurtful but can lead to reconciliation and love.

Names for Shiva

Shiva has different names and different forms, representing different aspects of Brahman. For example he is called

Mahayogi – The God of asceticism. Asceticism means giving up the good things of life and living a life as a holy man, meditating.

Nataraja – the Lord of the Dance. As Lord of the Dance, Shiva controls the universe.

Shiva as Lord of the Dance

Shiva as an ascetic

When looking at statues or posters of Shiva look out for the following symbols and think about what they say something about Shiva.

Symbol	Meaning
Shiva's four arms	A sign that Shiva is greater and more powerful than humans and can do many things at the same time. Shiva is powerful.
Hand drum	This shows that Shiva beats out the rhythm of life. He causes the pattern of day and night and the cycle of birth, death and rebirth. Shiva is in control of creation.
Flames of fire	Fire destroys, so the flames represent destruction. Shiva destroys in order to recreate.
Hand raised	This hand sign represents protection. Shiva protects.
Hand lowered	This hand sign represents action and salvation. Shiva acts to save life from disaster.
Snake Garland	The snake is a symbol of fertility and strength. Shiva creates.
Foot on dwarf	The dwarf represents ignorance, and Shiva's foot is stamping out ignorance. Shiva destroys evil and ignorance.
Dancing	Shiva is dancing with great energy and power. A dance represents life.

❶ Look carefully at the image of Shiva, as Lord of the Dance. Identify and label as many symbols as you can.

❷ Look carefully at the image of Shiva as the God of asceticism. Identify and label as many symbols as you can.

❸ What is asceticism? Find out about the importance of asceticism in Hinduism.

❹ In groups, carry out research into the goddess Lakshmi or the goddess Durga. Present a report of your findings which includes a statement about why you think they are important within Hinduism. The following website might help get you started – www.hindunet.com

❺ From the table of symbols and meanings list those which relate to creation.

MAKING CONNECTIONS

❶ What kinds of things do you like to make? Take into class something that you have created and that you are proud of. Include it in a class display.

❷ In groups, find out about some inventors. What was particularly creative about their work?

❸ Find out what science has to say about how the world came about.

❹ Describe a situation you have experienced or have knowledge about in which creation arose out of destruction.

❺ Describe a situation in your life or in the life of your school or community in which you would like to see creation emerging out of destruction. How hopeful are you that this will happen? Is there anything that you personally can do?

Thinking it over

❶ What does it mean to create? Is creating more than just making? Can you give examples of each?

❷ In groups discuss how you would go about creating a better society. Look through newspapers and magazines to identify the things you think ought to be changed. Then consider what changes you would like to see and what needs to happen for these changes to take effect. Present a report to the class.

❸ Was the world created or did it come about by chance? What evidence is there to support your view?

stimulus

4 *Puja at home*

Puja is the act of showing reverence and devotion to a God through prayers and rituals. In puja, Hindus involve all their senses and use water, light and fire in their rituals.

Water washes and cleans. It is a sign of trying to be clean and fit to appear before God.

Fire destroys, purifies and warms. It is a sign of the comfort of worship and thinking about the destruction of all that is wrong and trying to be more pure.

Light overcomes darkness, bringing light to dark places. It is a sign of overcoming the darkness of evil and ignorance.

Home shrine

Puja tray

12-year-old Meena describes morning puja at her home:

In our house we have set aside a corner in a room as a shrine. The shrine is a special place for us where we worship every day. My mum says that through our daily puja we are honouring and showing devotion and love to God. We are also, she says, being thankful because we have a lot to be thankful for.

On our shrine we have pictures and statues of some of our gods. We have pictures of Rama and Sita, a statue of the God Vishnu and my favourite, the elephant-headed God, Ganesha. Also on the shrine we have a special tray made from stainless steel, called the puja tray. We use this every morning to help us with our puja. We get up each morning about 7.00 and have a shower. We have to be clean for puja – not just our bodies but our minds as well. Then we meet together as a family at the

shrine to celebrate puja. My mum looks after the household shrine and she makes sure everything is ready for morning puja.

As we approach the shrine, we bow our heads as a sign of respect. On the tray there's a little handbell and the first thing is to ring the bell to tell everybody, including our gods, that it is time for puja. The sound of the bell is a signal for us to concentrate and put thoughts about school and homework out of our mind. In our worship we are showing devotion to our gods, so we take water from a pot on the puja tray to wash our statues. As a sign of respect we mark the forehead of the statues with a red powder. We then dress our statues and offer them flowers and food like fruits, rice, nuts and milk. On the puja tray is a container which holds joss sticks, so we light them and offer our statues the sweet smell of the incense. Just as the smell goes everywhere, this reminds us that

God is everywhere. We also have a special lamp on the tray called an arti lamp. Each of us passes our hands over the lighted lamp then over our forehead. As puja proceeds we say prayers and then towards the end we share the food we have offered to the statues. We have given it to them and now we receive it from them.

I think this is a good way to the start the day as a family. It takes us about 15–20 minutes, and puja is asking God's blessing for the day ahead and that we we will have a good, peaceful day. After puja it's time for breakfast and then off to school.

Key values in puja are:

- showing love, respect and devotion to God
- being thankful
- thinking about the evils and wrongs which need destroying
- starting the day as a family in a good way
- making sure a person is clean physically and clean spiritually.

❶ Draw a puja tray and mark on the main items.

❷ Show how the rituals involved in puja involve all the senses – touch, smell, sight, hearing and taste.

❸ Describe how fire, light and water are all used in puja. What do they signify?

❹ In what way is puja both about giving and receiving?

❺ Why do you think Meena believes that puja is a good way to start the day?

❻ Find out about the god Ganesha. Why do you think he is Meena's favourite?

❼ Which of the values associated with puja do you think would be most relevant to someone Meena's age? Why?

stimulus 5 *The mandir*

A mandir is a Hindu temple. In the United Kingdom many Hindu mandirs are converted houses or churches. The stimulus below gives some of the answers to questions that a class asked a Hindu when he made a visit to their school.

What is a mandir?

A mandir is a temple. It is the Hindu name for a place of worship or prayer. The name mandir actually comes from a Sanskrit (an ancient Hindu language in India) word for a place where the mind becomes still and the soul (atman) tries to seek the source of life, peace, joy and comfort.

Are there many mandirs in the United Kingdom?

I'm not sure how many there are. Many of our big cities have mandirs. In India, of course, there are thousands. In the United Kingdom many of our mandirs are converted houses or churches. It costs a lot of money to build a mandir. There is a very impressive purpose-built mandir in London – the Shri Swaminarayan Mandir.

Why do Hindus go to the mandir?

What do you find in a mandir?

Well, an easy answer is to say Hindus go to see the images, and show devotion to God. But I once read an explanation that made a lot of sense to me. This person wrote that we need schools to educate the mind. We need hospitals to heal the body when it is damaged in some way. We have cinemas and other places of entertainment to excite the mind. But where do we go to find peace of mind? So when we go to the mandir we are trying to get closer to God and focus our thoughts on God. Looking at our images helps us do this.

The most important room in the mandir is the main shrine room, where we have the images of our gods. In fact a mandir is regarded as home to the images. Your teacher told me you have done some work on our gods so you will remember that the images are not God, they represent the spirit of God. We have several images of gods, but most mandirs will focus especially on one god such as Shiva or Vishnu. We have other rooms as well for meetings and social activities.

Do you have ministers and priests?

At the mandir I attend we do have a priest. It's his job to look after our deities and offer puja at certain times each day. He is a very well educated man and knows a lot about our Hindu Scriptures.

Do you have regular times for worship?

As you know, many Hindu families offer puja every day at their home shrine. Going to the mandir is something we do often as individuals. We don't need others to go at the same time. However, in the United Kingdom we do have regular time together on a Sunday. This is because the mandir is like a centre for the Hindu Community and it is good to meet together regularly. We always get together as well at the time of our major festival celebrations like Diwali.

London (Neasden) Mandir

What about visits? Do you allow school pupils to visit the mandir?

Actually we welcome it. We think it is good that young people see what we do and learn more about Hinduism. Why don't you get your teacher to make arrangements? Just one or two things you'll need to bear in mind. Our mandir is important to us – as I said earlier it's a special place. This means that we expect people to come in appropriate dress – no short skirts or shorts. Also we will ask you to take your shoes off before entering our main shrine area. A couple of other things, whilst you are there it might be that some of our community will be offering puja – so make sure your mobile is switched off. Also if you are out for the day we would expect you to leave your sandwiches on the bus. As Hindus we will not have meat on the premises – and that would include fish and eggs. I'm sorry if all this sounds like a lot of don'ts but it is a sacred place to us. We'd be very pleased to see you though!

What are the important buildings in your community?

FINDING OUT

❶ Why are many mandirs converted houses or churches in the United Kingdom?

❷ Explain why Hindus think it important to go to the mandir.

❸ What is the role of a Hindu priest at the mandir?

❹ Find out more about the purpose-built mandir in London by visiting www.mandir.org. Write a brief report about what you find, especially about puja and about other activities organised at the mandir.

❺ Imagine you are an RE teacher. Write a letter to parents, saying you are taking your class on a visit to a local mandir. In your letter explain why you are going, and give advice about dress, mobile phones and food, which pupils will need to take note of.

❻ In the stimulus it is argued that people need places where they can find peace of mind. What is 'peace of mind'? Discuss this in groups and report your conclusions to the class.

MAKING CONNECTIONS

❶ Share times you have visited a religious building as part of an educational visit. Where did you go? Why did you go? What did you learn?

❷ In the stimulus it is argued that all communities need schools, hospitals, places of entertainment and places of worship. What do you think are the important buildings in your community? Why are they important?

❸ Conduct a survey in your community of places of worship. If there is a Hindu temple find out as much as you can about it.

❹ Do you have a special place where you go to find peace of mind? What is special about it? Can you describe it? Does it work?

❺ Does your school have such a place? If not, do you think it would be a good idea? How should such a place be set out? What name would you give to it?

❻ Would you say you have peace of mind? What kind if things can disturb your peace of mind? Can you give an example?

Judaism

Yom Kippur

Yom Kippur, meaning the Day of Atonement, is the most important day in the Jewish year. It is a day of fasting when Jews ask G-d for forgiveness. Judaism says that if a person has not forgiven his or her neighbour then he or she cannot expect G-d to forgive them. So, in the days before Yom Kippur, Jews are expected to seek forgiveness from their relatives and friends for any wrong they may have done them.

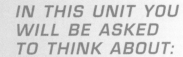

IN THIS UNIT YOU WILL BE ASKED TO THINK ABOUT:

✓ GUILT
✓ RECONCILIATION
✓ PROMISES
✓ SELF-DISCIPLINE
✓ FORGIVENESS

stimulus 1 *Preparing for Yom Kippur*

The day itself is very special, but like any special day you need to get ready for it.

3 days to Yom Kippur	*Visit Auntie Rachel. Tell her I'm sorry for making nippy comments about her chicken soup. Remember, she thinks she's being helpful…*	
2 days to Yom Kippur	*Do a round of family visits. Make sure everything's OK with everyone…*	

	Speak to David who I fell out with at the swimming club. It was partly my fault – ask his forgiveness.	
Erev Yom Kippur	Have a good meal to stock up for the fast ahead.	
	Write a cheque for charity – make it a bit more than usual.	
	Have a good bath in the mikvah.	
	Iron white gowns and sort out Tallith.	
Yom Kippur	Attend all services.	

FINDING OUT

❶ Why is this person going to say sorry to Aunt Rachel?

❷ Why is this person intending to have a big meal on the night before Yom Kippur?

❸ Find out as much as you can about the mikvah and what it symbolises.

❹ Draw a tallith and explain when and by whom it is worn.

❺ Why do you think a white gown is often worn at Yom Kippur?

stimulus 2 *Why is Yom Kippur special?*

At Yom Kippur I try to put the year behind me – well, all the bad stuff anyway! Life's a tricky thing sometimes; you just don't always get it right with people – especially the ones closest to you. In fact it's sometimes even more difficult with them. Yom Kippur forces me to face up to myself. Sometimes I don't like what I see, but Yom Kippur gives me a way to fix it for the year ahead. I don't really go to the synagogue any other time. You'd think the ones who do would be quite happy to see me feel guilty, but they don't. That's because we all know that we've not lived up to what we should throughout the year – well not to G-d's standards anyway. I'm welcomed with open arms and that feels really great – like coming home. Forgiving others isn't always easy, and being forgiven for what you've done can't always be easy for people to do back, but you do it. That's the way it is. When you've done that, G-d forgives you too. Even if you don't think you've done much that's all that bad, that's a big weight off your shoulders….

Benjamin

❶ What does Benjamin try to do at Yom Kippur? What does he mean?

❷ What do you think he means by 'you just don't always get it right with people'?

❸ 'Yom Kippur forces me to face up to myself. Sometimes I don't like what I see'. Explain what Benjamin means by this.

❹ Why does he feel Yom Kippur is like 'coming home'?

❺ What is meant by the phrase 'a big weight off your shoulders'?

MAKING CONNECTIONS

❶ When did you last fall out with someone? How did you make up? If you haven't, what is stopping you?

❷ Think about the year which has just passed. Write about the things which you wish hadn't happened – especially those which you had control over. Now write about how you'd like next year to be different and how you're going to make it better.

❸ Have you ever looked at yourself and not liked what you saw?

❹ Describe a time when you have felt a 'weight coming off your shoulders'.

❺ Can you describe a time when you felt guilty? How did it feel?

❻ In groups, make a list of things you might feel guilty about.

Thinking it over

❶ Do you think you fall out with the people closest to you more than anyone else? Why might this be?

❷ Why do you think people sometimes find it hard to 'face up to themselves'? What kinds of things are people often unhappy with themselves about? What should they do about it?

❸ What does the word reconciliation mean? How hard should you try to make up with someone you have fallen out with? Does it depend on who it is? Why or why not?

❹ When trying to make up for what you have done, are actions sometimes more important than words? Can you give an example?

❺ What is the difference between breaking a rule and doing something you know is wrong? Which is likely to make you feel more guilty?

stimulus 3 · *What happens during Yom Kippur?*

After a good meal on the eve of Yom Kippur, Jewish families attend the first service in the synagogue. This is known as Kol Nidre, meaning 'all vows'. Synagogues are usually very full for this service. All the scrolls are taken out of the Ark and the Kol Nidre prayer is sung three times. The prayer is a plea for G-d's forgiveness. During the next day there are long services in the synagogue with virtually no break until nightfall. Services will often begin around 7.30 in the morning and finish around 7pm. Yom Kippur is a day of fasting when Jews abstain from food and drink for 25 hours so a good deal of self-control is required. The Torah will be read at both the morning and the afternoon services including passages from the Book of Leviticus. In the afternoon service the Book of Jonah is also read. The services conclude with the blowing of the shofar. Yom Kippur is over. Hopefully G-d has forgiven our sins, we can hope for a good year to come.

(Adapted from Rabbi Douglas Charing, *Six World Faiths*)

FINDING OUT

❶ What is the 'shofar' and what role does it play in Yom Kippur?

❷ What is Kol Nidre and why is it such an important part of Yom Kippur?

❸ Why is a good deal of self-control required on Yom Kippur?

stimulus 4 · *The Kol Nidre*

The Kol Nidre is a sung prayer about the vows, oaths and promises a Jewish person makes to G-d. It is important because it shows Jewish people they have a new start at Yom Kippur.

All vows, oaths and promises which we made to G-d between last Yom Kippur to this one and weren't able to keep – may all these between us and G-d be cancelled. May they be void and of no effect. May we be forgiven for them and released from them. They should not be considered vows or oaths or promises.

Kol Nidrey ve-esarey va-ha-ramey v'konamey v'hinu-yey v'kinusey u-sh'vuot, di-n'darna u-d'ish-t'vana, u-d'ah-rimna, v'di-asarna al naf-sha-tana mi-yom kipurim sheh-avar ad yom kipurim zeh ha-ba aleynu l'tovah, kol-hon ih-ratna v'hon, kol-hon y'hon sharan. Sh'vikin, sh'vitin, b'teylin u-m'vutalin, la sh'ririn v'la ka-yamin Nidrana la nidrey, ve-esarana la esarey, u-sh'vuatana la sh'vuot.

① What does the Kol Nidre say about the promises and vows made by a Jew and G-d?

② Why is Yom Kippur like a new start for Jewish people?

MAKING CONNECTIONS

① Try to listen to a recording of the Kol Nidre. Describe the sound. Is it a happy or sad sound? What does it make you feel?

② What songs make you thoughtful? Do you have a special song which you think of as 'yours'? Do your parents? What songs do you associate with certain times? What kinds of things go through your mind when you hear them (for example, Auld Lang Syne at Hogmanay)?

③ The Kol Nidre is about keeping and breaking promises, vows and oaths. What is the most important and serious promise you have ever made. Who did you make it to? Why? Did you keep it? If you didn't, how did you feel?

Singing Auld Lang Syne to celebrate the New Year

5 Fasting

> 'The following regulations are to be observed for all time to come. On the tenth day of the seventh month the Israelites and the foreigners living among them must fast and must not do any work. On that day the ritual is to be performed to purify them from all their sins, so that they will be ritually clean.'
>
> (Leviticus 16:29–30)

Four main reasons are given for fasting:

- It is a way of showing that the desire for forgiveness is genuine.
- Fasting requires self-discipline and it is thought that this helps the individual become a better person.
- If the physical needs of the body are ignored for a day, it is easier for people to concentrate on their spiritual needs.
- Fasting can make a person more compassionate and sensitive to the needs of others.

① As well as fasting, what must Jews not do on the Day of Atonement?

② Why do these actions need self-discipline? What is self-discipline?

③ What do people mean when they talk about a person's
a. physical needs
b. spiritual needs?

Thinking it over

❶ Do you think that you have good self-discipline? Can you give examples which show strong and weak self-discipline? Can you think of any ways in which people could improve their self-discipline?

❷ Is it sometimes difficult to control your actions? Can you give examples? What is self-control? Is it a good thing? Why?

❸ Do you agree that fasting will help people to concentrate on their spiritual needs? How? Is it only religious people that have spiritual needs or do all people have them? How else, apart from fasting, might someone focus on their spiritual needs?

We confess that we have…

Hardened our hearts
Spoken in ways we shouldn't
Harmed our neighbour
Been unpleasant to parents and teachers
Jumped to conclusions
Lied and denied
Taken bribes
Made fun of others
Called people names
Been dishonest with money
Eaten and drunk too much
Taken money for nothing
Been full of ourselves
Gossiped
Looked at others down our nose
Ignored the Commandments
Argued about nothing
Put people in difficult situations
Been jealous of others
Been flippant about serious things
Been inflexible
Told tales
Made empty promises
Hated people for no reason
Broken promises
Not thought about what we were doing
Broken laws
Tried to keep our sins secret from you.
(*Authorised Daily Prayer Book*)

stimulus
6 Confessions

Before starting the New Year off in the best possible way, things that have been done wrong in the past year must be confessed. This is called viduy. It is always said as '*we* …' because it is confession on behalf of all Jews. As well as these spoken confessions, each individual person should confess their own wrongs to G-d.

1 Of this list of confessions, which do you think is the worst thing?

2 Choose five of the confessions at random. In groups, rank these in order of seriousness. Be prepared to support your point of view.

3 Find out what people mean by the following:
- hardening your heart
- being inflexible
- looking at people down your nose
- being flippant.

MAKING CONNECTIONS

1 Go through the list of confessions and choose two of the statements. Now, answer the following questions about each statement *in relation to yourself*.
a. When did I last do this?
b. Why did I do it?
c. Who could have been (or was) harmed by it and how?
d. How could I avoid doing this again?

2 Describe a time when you have been on the receiving end of any of these wrong things. What happened? What did it feel like?

 7 *The story of Jonah*

The story of Jonah is read at Yom Kippur. *You should have a narrator read this story in class and work out a silent drama to go with it.*

One day, the Lord spoke to Jonah, son of Amittai. He said, 'Go to Nineveh, that great city, and speak out against it; I am aware how wicked its people are.' Jonah, however, set out in the opposite direction in order to get away from the Lord. He went to Joppa, where he found a ship about to go to Spain. He paid his fare and went aboard with the crew to sail to Spain, where he would be away from the Lord.

(Jonah 1:1–3)

G-d sent a powerful storm which scared the sailors silly. Jonah sneaked off below decks and hid (again), but the sailors found him.

'We think G-d's after you! That's why this big storm is here – G-d's come for you and we're going to pay for whatever you've done to get him so annoyed!'

And Jonah admitted (more or less) that all this was true.

Jonah was caught between the angry men and the deep blue sea – so he decided to take his chances with the ocean.

'Throw me overboard, then G-d will calm down and give up with the storm'. So they did. The storm ended – what a relief!

Now G-d was annoyed but he likes to give people a chance. So he had a very large fish swallow Jonah. But he must have done something to its digestion because Jonah stayed inside it for three days and nights – even if he did start to smell a bit.

Jonah said a long and powerful prayer to say sorry to G-d. He realised his mistake and promised to make amends for it. So, with one almighty burp the fish brought Jonah up and spat him out onto dry land. Jonah now agreed to go to Nineveh and remind them how G-d wanted them to behave. When he finally reached Nineveh he proclaimed to the people:

'You lot, you've got forty days to clean up your act or G-d is really going to make you wish you weren't here. Trust me, I know what I'm talking about' (He'd tell the story of why he smelled so fishy later).

The King of Nineveh heard this and believed Jonah. So he instructed the city to sort itself out. From now on, everyone would live a good, honest life. And the people did what they were told. So, G-d decided to let them be. Now, funnily enough, Jonah was kind of annoyed about this – and decided he'd rather be dead. G-d asked him what he was so grumpy about and said to him:

'There are more than 120,000 people in that city – not to mention all the animals – why shouldn't I take pity on them when they have turned away from their evil ways?'

❶ Why and how did Jonah run away from G-d?

❷ Why did Jonah offer to let them throw him overboard?

❸ How did G-d save Jonah from drowning?

❹ Why do you think Jonah changed his mind about going to Nineveh?

❺ Why do you think Jonah was so annoyed when the people of Nineveh repented and changed their ways?

❻ As a class, make a wall frieze of the story of Jonah. Each group should take a different part of the story – be as creative as you can.

❼ What beliefs about G-d are contained in the story of Jonah?

❽ Why do you think the story of Jonah is read at Yom Kippur?

MAKING CONNECTIONS

❶ Do you find it easy or difficult to admit you are wrong and say sorry? Why do you think this is? Think of as many reasons as you can about why some people might find forgiveness a difficult thing to do.

❷ Describe a time when you have forgiven or been forgiven.

❸ Make a 'forgiveness-o-meter'. Draw up a list of things in your class which would need forgiveness. Now make up a reaction thermometer. At the top put 'impossible to forgive' and at the bottom put 'easy to forgive'. Read out the statements in class and move the thermometer up and down according to what the class says.

❹ How do you feel if someone says sorry but you know they don't mean it?

❺ Have you ever felt you wanted to make a new start – with parents, brothers, sisters, or friends? What did you do?

❻ Describe someone who you think has changed for the better. It could be someone you know or have read about.

❼ Listen to the song 'Sorry seems to be the hardest word' by Elton John. What is this song about? Do you agree with it?

❽ Write you own short story about forgiveness (or lack of it!).

Thinking it over

❶ Did the people of Nineveh get off too lightly? What do you think?

❷ Are there some things that should never be forgiven? If so, what and why?

❸ Is it easier to forgive than to forget? Why or why not? Why do you think people sometimes do wrong things even when they know it's wrong?

❹ Is the picture of G-d found in the story of Jonah an acceptable one as far as you are concerned? What beliefs do you find acceptable or unacceptable?

❺ Is forgiveness an important part of human life or is it just for 'religious' people? Give reasons for your answer.

Esther

The book of Esther in the Hebrew Bible tells the story of how the Jews were saved from persecution and death. It is the story of one woman's courage and the triumph of good over evil. Instead of keeping quiet Esther speaks out to save others, but in doing so risks her own life. The story is set in Persia (present day Iran) around 470BCE. It is read in the synagogue each year at the Festival of Purim.

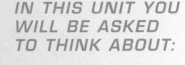

IN THIS UNIT YOU WILL BE ASKED TO THINK ABOUT:

✓ COURAGE

✓ HATRED

✓ GOOD AND EVIL

✓ TAKING RISKS

✓ PLEASURE

stimulus 1 What is good, and what is bad?

'It's always clear who the good guys are and who the bad guys are.'

'I'm good at maths but I'm not very good at history.'

'Something can be called good if you mean well.'

'There are some things which are always evil and some things which are always good.'

'If someone kicks you, you've got to kick them back, haven't you? It's obvious.'

'I love cheeseburger meals but I know they're not very good for me.'

'What's good and what's bad depends on your point of view.'

'Something is good if it ends up with a good result.'

MAKING CONNECTIONS

1 Make a chart listing the good things in your life on one side and the bad things on the other. Are there things that fall in the middle? What are they?

2 Make another chart this time showing things that are 'good for you' and things that are 'bad for you'.

3 Write a report on yourself detailing what you are good at and what you are not so good at.

4 Design a poster in your class using images from newspapers and magazines. On one side should be images representing good and on the other side those representing evil.

5 Identify stories and films in which the struggle between good and evil is an important element. In each case describe what the struggle is about.

 2 *The story of Esther*

Thinking it over

1 What do 'good' and 'bad' mean? From the 'making connections' activities above describe the different ways in which the words 'good' and 'bad' can be used.

2 Would you describe natural disasters such as the Asian Tsunami and diseases such as AIDS as evil? Or is evil something that is caused deliberately by human beings, such as war?

3 Do you agree that it is always clear what's good and what's evil? How can you tell the difference between them?

4 Is there anything which you think is always wrong, no matter what the circumstances?

5 Do you think taking revenge is a good thing?

6 What's more important when you try to do something good – that you mean well or that it ends up with a good result?

The Characters

Ahasuersus

Job: King
Role: Makes all the important decisions
Comment: A bit changeable, especially after some wine. Don't get too close to him. You never know what he'll do next. Seems to have let the power go to his head. Catch him in a good mood and you might be lucky – or not!

Esther

Job: Beautiful Jewish girl who becomes Queen
Role: Hatches a plan to save all the Jews
Comment: A courageous girl. Risks the King's anger to save others – could have lost her head here, but instead kept it by being way too clever for everyone else!

Haman

Job: King's Prime Minister and Chief Adviser
Role: Plans the extermination of the Jews, who he hates
Comment: An evil man who works his way into the King's affections and then misuses his power for his own wicked reasons.

Mordechai

Job: Esther's foster-father and one of the King's courtiers
Role: Gives Esther advice and stands up to Haman
Comment: Fearful of the danger Esther is in but supports her plan.

The Story

Hi, my name is Esther. You might have heard of me. I ended up as the Queen of all Persia. They wrote about me and put this in the Holy Book of my people – what an honour! But I was only doing what I knew in my heart was right. Wouldn't you have done the same? What is my story? Well, let me tell you…

Ahasuersus was the mighty King of Persia, but sometimes he had a bit too much to drink and got a bit grumpy. Once when he was like this he pretty much fell out with his wife, Queen Vashti. She embarrassed him in public and he was really not chuffed about it. So, he decided to replace her. Now he did this by holding a beauty contest and so I ended up in the palace along with others to be selected (or not). My foster dad, Mordechai – he'd brought me up after my parents died – worked at the palace, he made sure I was OK. Now, they kept us in the palace for a year making us fit for Ahasuersus – honestly! I'm not a big fan of make-up, so I didn't really bother with it – but I think that was what won the King over in the end. Some of the others looked like painted dolls – which actually made them look a bit weird. Anyway, I became Queen.

Now, I didn't tell you yet – I'm a Jew. I didn't tell Ahasuersus either – Mordechai said it would be better not to. We Jews had ended up in Persia and sometimes things weren't all that good for us – so when I became Queen I thought I should maybe carry on keeping this quiet.

Now I have to tell you about Haman – what a total creep he was. He hated the Jews, I still don't know why. But what did Ahasuersus go and do? Only promote Haman to a powerful position in the palace. Haman asked for everyone to bow before him, but Mordechai wouldn't (good for him!). Haman was really mad about that – so he took his chance to get back at all the Jews – and persuaded Ahasuersus that all the Jews were a threat to his kingdom, because they didn't follow his laws. What rubbish! I'm a Jew and I followed the laws – I even married Ahasuersus because he commanded it, for godness sake! Haman was really superstitious. He drew lots called Purim to decide when the Jews should all die. Mordechai couldn't believe all of this and more or less gave up – reminding me that I, too, would die if Ahasuersus found out I was a Jew. But I ignored this and hatched a plan.

You can only appear before the King if he commands it – if he hasn't he might just have you killed. But I had to take the risk and go and see him without his permission. I had to save the Jews. I had to save my own people. I had to stop Haman. Now don't ask me why, but Ahasuersus accepted me and listened to my request. I decided that he had

to know I was a Jew and that all the Jews should be spared because they, just like me, did follow the rule of Ahasuersus. But I knew how to butter him up, so I invited him and Haman to dinner. I knew what I was doing. Meanwhile, Haman had a gallows built to hang Mordechai but when Ahasuersus heard that Mordechai had once saved him from being attacked by two of his own guards, he made Haman reward Mordechai – I loved that bit. You should have seen Haman's face then! At the meal I had prepared – with plenty of Ahasuersus' favourite wine, I took the biggest risk of all. He told me he would grant me anything I asked. So I told him. 'Ahasuersus I am a Jew. If you allow all the Jews to be killed, then I too must die'. Ahasuersus went white as a sheet. But not as white as Haman. Ahasuersus looked at Haman and roared with anger. He turned to his guards. 'Take Haman and hang him on the gallows he has prepared for Mordechai, NOW!' And they did. The King then appointed Mordechai as chief steward in Haman's place. So we Jews were saved.

FINDING OUT

1 How did Esther come to be Queen of Persia?

2 How did Esther succeed in saving the situation? Why was she courageous?

3 Describe Mordechai's part in the story.

4 In the story Esther was very courageous. Research the life of someone in the past or present whom you believe to be a 'woman of courage'.

5 Courage is sometimes referred to as a virtue? What is a virtue? What other virtues are there?

MAKING CONNECTIONS

❶ What's the bravest thing you have ever done? Write about this, showing what you did and why. Write about what was going through your mind during this and afterwards.

❷ Who is the bravest person you know? In what way are they brave?

❸ Conduct an interview with or read an account by someone whose job involves courage, for example: a firefighter or police officer. Do they see themselves as being courageous?

❹ Is everyone scared sometimes? What are you most afraid of? Are there good reasons to be afraid of it?

Lisa Potts was awarded the George Medal for bravery after her nursery class was attacked by a man with a machete

Thinking it over

❶ Can you show courage and still be afraid?

❷ People often show courage when facing danger. At what other times do you need courage?

❸ Can people be brave without knowing it?

❹ Do you think you are more courageous now than you were when you were younger? Why?

❺ Is everyone capable of being brave? Do you think you can learn to be brave?

stimulus 3

Haman's plot

The extract on page 65 is from the Jewish Bible. It is part of the story of Esther. It focuses on the time Mordechai disobeyed the King and refused to show respect to Haman, and Haman took the opportunity to plot against the Jews. Read the extract before attempting the Finding Out questions below.

❶ How did Haman expect to be treated by his officials?

❷ Why did Mordechai refuse to treat him in this way?

❸ How did Haman react when he found out? What did he decide to do?

❹ What reasons did Haman give the King for killing all the Jews in the Empire?

❺ What financial guarantee did Haman offer the King to make sure he went along with his plan?

❻ How would you describe Haman's actions?

Some time later the King promoted a man named Haman to the position of prime minister… The king ordered all the officials in his service to show respect for Haman by kneeling and bowing to him. They all did so except Mordechai, who refused to do it. The other officials in the royal service asked him why he was disobeying the king's command; day after day they urged him to give in, but he would not listen to them. 'I am a Jew', he explained, 'and I cannot bow to Haman.' So they told Haman about this, wondering if he would tolerate Mordechai's conduct. Haman was furious when he realised that Mordechai was not going to kneel and bow to him, and when he learnt that Mordechai was a Jew, he decided to do more than punish Mordechai alone. He made plans to kill every Jew in the whole Persian empire…

So Haman told the king, 'There is a certain race of people scattered all over your empire and found in every province. They observe customs that are not like any other people. Moreover, they do not obey the laws of the empire so it is not in your best interests to tolerate them. If it please your majesty, issue a decree that they are to be put to death. If you do, I guarantee that I will be able to put more than 340,000 kilograms of silver into the royal treasury for the administration of the empire.' The king took off his ring, which was used to stamp proclamations and make them official, and gave it to the enemy of the Jewish people… The king told him, 'The people and their money are yours; do as you like with them.'

(Esther 3:1–11)

Thinking it over

1 Why do you think Haman hated Mordechai and the Jews so much that he wanted to kill them?

2 What kind of feelings do you think give rise to hatred? Do you think hatred can ever be a good thing?

3 How bad does something have to be before it can be described as evil?

4 Do people have to be a certain age before they can know that they are doing something evil?

5 Will there always be evil? Do you think that people who do evil can be changed to do good?

6 In the story of Esther good defeats evil. Do you think good will always defeat evil?

7 Have human beings become better or worse since the time of Esther? What evidence would you offer to support your view?

8 Are we allowed to do anything in order to get rid of evil? In other words, does the end justify the means?

stimulus
4 *The festival of Purim*

Haman ordered lots to be cast ('purim' they were called) to find out the right day and month to carry out his plot. The thirteenth day of the twelfth month, the month of Adar, was decided on.

(Esther 3:7)

Purim is celebrated by Jews each year on the 14th of the month of Adar (February/March) It is a joyful time. One of the main parts of the celebration is the reading of the Megillah – the hand-written scroll of the Book of Esther. As this is done, children (and adults!) stamp their feet and make loud noises every time the name of Haman is mentioned. This reminds them of the story, has the effect of blotting out Haman's name and is also good fun!

There is a great meal on Purim to celebrate. People are even allowed to get drunk, but not too drunk! In fact, it is a mitzvah (rule) to have wine and be merry! Special foods are eaten on Purim like hamantashen. These are little pastries filled with hidden ingredients like jam. They are three-cornered in shape, some say to represent Haman's hat, others say it was the shape of his ears! The idea of things hidden reminds Jews that although the name of G-d is not even mentioned in the Book of Esther, Jews believe that G-d is nevertheless there, hidden behind it all, bringing about the victory of good over evil.

In modern Israel there are processions through the streets and floats bearing images of all the leading characters. Children dress up in fancy dress, reminding them of how Esther initially disguised the fact that she was a Jew. People exchange presents and give to the poor. This reminds them of the great gift Esther gave in risking her own life for her fellow Jews.

A street procession during the festival of Purim

FINDING OUT

❶ How did the festival of Purim get its name?

❷ What happens when Haman's name is mentioned while the story of Esther is being read out in the synagogue? Why?

❸ How is Purim celebrated in modern Israel?

❹ What are hamantashen and what are they said to represent?

❺ Although Jews are allowed to get (almost) drunk on Purim, some are not. Find out who and why.

MAKING CONNECTIONS

❶ Have a Purim celebration in class. Read the Esther story out – or present it in some other way (for example, a play with masks) and make lots of noise when Haman's name is mentioned!

❷ Are there any foods you eat at different times of year which have a symbolic meaning? Make a list of them – perhaps you could have a tasting session in your class.

❸ Purim is a joyful time. What do you enjoy doing most?

❹ Is it important that your family and friends enjoy doing the same things as you? Why or why not?

❺ What kinds of things have you been told not to take risks with? Have you always obeyed these warnings? Give an example of when you ignored the warnings. What does this tell you about yourself?

Thinking it over

❶ How important is it for people to enjoy themselves and celebrate together?

❷ Is there any difference between enjoying yourself and being happy?

❸ Do pleasure and enjoyment make for a happy and fulfilling life? What else do you think is required?

❹ 'Life is short, enjoy it while you can.' Do you agree?

❺ Can the pursuit of pleasure and enjoyment sometimes involve taking risks? Can you give examples?

❻ Esther risked her life. Do you think anything is worth risking your life for?

❼ Why do you think Jews remember the story of Esther every year?

Suffering

This unit is based mainly on the Book of Job in the Hebrew Bible. It focuses on the difficult question of suffering in human life and how we should respond to it. The unit also looks at the history of suffering within Judaism and in particular, at the Holocaust and its impact on Jewish religion.

IN THIS UNIT YOU WILL BE ASKED TO THINK ABOUT:

✓ SUFFERING

✓ ACCEPTANCE

✓ PATIENCE

✓ REBELLION

✓ HOPE

stimulus 1 Types of suffering

What does it mean to suffer? Are some kinds of suffering worse than others?

1. Oh this is soooo boring… Another sticky hot day in this school. Teachers droning on about stuff I don't understand and don't care about anyway. I've got superswot next to me with all the answers. I just don't get it. Why do I have to be here? Why can't I just stay at home and watch TV? What's the point – it's all soooo dull…

2. I haven't got much time left. I just wish there wasn't so much pain. So many drugs but they don't help. It'll all be over soon anyway. The pain I can cope with, but I'll not see my kids grow up. So much despair. Why me?

3. All they see is the homeless guy sitting on the ground. No, I'm not a con-man. These few coins are for my next meal – not drugs or drink. I have some self-respect left. Why do people think they can look at me that way? They're lucky and I'm not – why does that make them think they're better than me?

4. Asian Tsunami
9/11
Bali
Moscow
Iraq
Bhopal
Rwanda
Sudan
Belfast
Clydebank
Armenia
Lockerbie

MAKING CONNECTIONS

❶ Many songs are about feeling low and going through hard times. Think of the lyrics of one song you know like this. Write out these lyrics and explain what they're trying to say. Explain whether you agree with them or not and why.

❷ Write about a time when you experienced suffering of some kind. At the end of this piece of writing, write about how you managed to cope with it. Destroy this piece of writing afterwards if you like.

❶ In what ways is the person in 1 suffering?

❷ What kinds of suffering is the person in 2 going through?

❸ How might the person in 3 be suffering?

❹ Find out about one of the references in 4. Write a report on your findings.

❺ Take four pieces of paper of different shapes and colours – from very dark to very light. On each write something which you would call suffering (use darker paper the more serious the suffering is). Now display these in class for people to look at. Put all the same or similar ideas together in groups. What comes up most and least often? In groups, make a note of all the ideas and order them from the most serious to the least serious. What differences are there between groups? Discuss and note down any interesting findings.

❻ Make a class collage of cut-out images to illustrate the idea of suffering. It can be a 3D design if you like. You could put your own artwork ideas inside.

2 The problem with suffering

For many people, the fact that there is suffering in the world can be used as an argument against the existence of G-d. After all, if there is a G-d, why would he let people suffer?

Rab and Donnie are on their lunch break. They're standing at Greasy Joe's Munchy Wagon waiting for their burgers…

Rab: Aw c'mon. Ah'm starvin'.
Donnie: Naw you're no.
Rab: AYE AH UM.
Donnie: NAW, You're NO. They people in war zones, they're starvin'. They people in famines, they're starvin'.
Rab: Look. Ye know what ah mean.
Donnie: Aye, well. Nae need tae overdo it is there?
Rab: It's aw G-d's fault anyway.
Donnie: (very puzzled) What are ye oan aboot noo, ya numpty?

Rab: Well, ah'm starvin', not tae mention cold and pretty skint the noo. So much for the Big Man in the Sky eh? No lookin' after me aw that well is he?
Donnie: Dae you really think that aw the almighty's got tae do aw day is make sure you've got a burger in your mooth and a pound in your pocket?
Rab: Naw, but he's no doin' much else is he?
Donnie: You've lost me now, ye really have…
Rab: Well, the great, good G-d.
Donnie: Whit's wi the G.-.D?
Rab: Och that's ma new mate Benjamin. He's Jewish. He tell me ye shouldny take G-d's name in vain.
Donnie: That'll cut your vocabulary doon tae aboot ten words then eh?
Rab: Aye, aye. Anyway. If there was a G-d, he canny be very good or very powerful if he lets so many bad things happen can he? Every day there's a new horror story in the papers. Whit's G-d doin' aboot it. No very much as far as I can see.
Donnie: The papers probably didny contact him for his comments
Rab: Funny man. But G-d doesny do anything tae stop sufferin' – so either he

canny or he disny want tae. Either way, it's no very nice is it?

The queue has moved forward and Rab and Donnie are now chewing on their burgers…

Donnie: Well, here's somethin'. What aboot all that pain and suffering you've got in your hand?

Rab looks at his burger… confused (him, not the burger) Then back at Donnie questioningly…

Donnie: I'll bet you've no idea how much cruelty went into raising that poor little future quarter-pounder. But you don't think aboot that do you? You just eat it. If you didny buy it no-one would make it – especially if ye didny want it for 75p. How else can they make it that cheap? You caused that bit of sufferin all by yourself. And while we're at it, in case you hudny noticed, we both work in a factory which makes bits for army tanks. What do you think they do with them? Take children for charity rides in them? Naw. They sometimes use them tae kill people. Pretty serious suffering that is by the way. And that wee screw which you so lovingly tightened will be right there makin' it aw work really smoothly.

Rab: So your sayin' it's ma fault.

Donnie: Ah'm sayin' it's no just G-d's fault.

Rab: Aw, just eat your burger will ye…

Although we believe in G-d's involvement in history, if we stop to ask why did this happen, we might come to accept tragedy instead of fighting against it. Judaism is an attempt not to ask why but, What should I do? How can I help? I don't think we can begin to ask why. The message is that we all belong together. We must put our efforts into saving life. We believe G-d needs our help to help those who suffer.

(Dr Jonathan Sacks, Chief Rabbi, on the Asian Tsunami)

FINDING OUT

❶ Make two lists – one of examples of suffering caused by people and one with examples caused by natural events.

❷ Why does Rab say he's starving and how does Donnie answer him?

❸ Explain why Rab thinks G-d's to blame for suffering.

❹ Donnie argues that suffering is not just G-d's fault. What point does he make?

❺ Explain the practical approach to suffering suggested by the Chief Rabbi, Dr Jonathan Sacks.

MAKING CONNECTIONS

❶ Think of the last time you did something you shouldn't have done. What did you do? Why? What harm might it have caused? Who might have suffered because of it? Is there anything you can do about it now?

❷ Have you ever had to suffer for something which you didn't actually do? How did you feel about it at the time? How do you feel about it now?

❸ What, if anything, can you, as an individual, do to help people who are suffering?

Thinking it over

❶ Do you agree with Rab's argument that if there is a G-d, he must be responsible for human suffering? Why or why not?

❷ Do you agree with Donnie's argument that G-d cannot be responsible for all suffering? Why or why not?

❸ Some people believe that G-d does not stop suffering because this would mean he would have to take away everyone's free choices. What do you think?

❹ Is the practical approach suggested by the Chief Rabbi the best approach or is it just a neat way of avoiding the question?

❺ Can any good ever come out of suffering or is suffering always a bad thing?

stimulus 3 · The suffering of Job

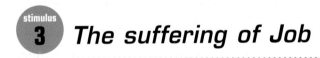

> There was a man in the land of Uz, whose name was Job; and that man was blameless and upright, one who feared G-d and turned away from evil.
>
> (Job 1:1)

Job had a great life. He was rich and well-respected. He was a fine businessman with herds of livestock and many workers. But it wouldn't last. His life was soon the opposite. Instead of being wealthy and happy he became poor, miserable and sick. So where did it all go wrong? Bandits from Sheba stole his livestock and killed his servants; lightning struck and killed all his sheep as well as the shepherds. Then more outlaws stole his camels and killed his other servants. Surely it couldn't get any worse? But it did. A storm came and killed his children. Job was miserable. While he was as down as anyone could be, he got a horrible disease. This covered his body in sores. He was so miserable he sat beside a rubbish-heap and scratched at them with an old bit of pottery.

At first Job accepted all his misfortunes without complaint. He refused to blame G-d. But what had he done to deserve all this? Nothing, as far as he knew. He had always lived a good life. Why had G-d suddenly become his enemy?

His friends came but instead of comforting him they accused him of being bad. Why else would he be suffering like this if he hadn't done something awful to deserve it? As far as his friends were concerned you get what you deserve. If you live a good life you will be rewarded but if you don't, you will be visited by terrible misfortunes, just like Job had been.

Job refused to accept his friends' point of view. He knew from his own experience that the innocent can be torn apart by tragic and meaningless suffering. He became angry and rebelled against G-d. If only he could break through to G-d and state his case surely all would be well.

Just when Job thought that he was grinding to his death, the G-d who he'd been calling on day and night… appeared! G-d answered Job. He reminded him of all the amazing things he does. He put Job right in his place by asking him a lot of questions which he could not answer As Job heard of all the things G-d had done, he started to question himself. 'What am I thinking of? G-d must know what he's doing. He always does. There must be a reason for all of this.

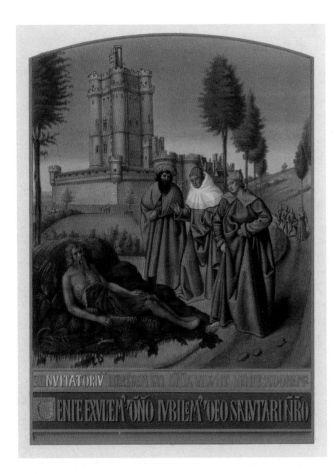

And the Lord restored the
fortunes of Job, when he had
prayed for his friends; and the
Lord gave Job twice as much as
he had before.

(Job 42:10)

Do I really need to know why?' Job realised
that there were no neat answers to the
question of suffering in human life but he
now knew that he could cope with G-d at his
side.

A minute with Job. Questions and answers with the man who got through what most of us wouldn't.

Q – Is it true you're from the land of Oz?

A – No, the land of Uz.

Q – What was your life like before the grim
stuff?

A – Great. Lovely kids, swanky house, loadsa
money. I suppose I had it all.

Q – What was the hardest thing?

A – The loss of the kids I guess.

Q – What about the boils?

A – They were everywhere. Absolutely
disgusting – weepy pus and bloody…

Q – Yes, thanks for that. Weren't you
annoyed with G-d?

A – Not at first. You see, you can't welcome
what G-d sends only when it's good. You
have to face up to everything that comes
your way. It's easy to follow G-d when
things are going well.

Q – So you cracked eventually?

A – I'm only human after all. Yes I was angry
with G-d. I went through the usual 'Why
me?' thing. Anyone would. But I still
believed. Even in anger I was angry with
G-d, I never turned it on anyone else.

Q – Do you think that helped?

A – Yeah I do. Even though I was being angry
I didn't give up hope. I didn't think that
my misery proved there wasn't a G-d. I
knew he was there but I just didn't get it.

Q – But G-d did answer you eventually,
didn't he?

A – Yes. Things are great now, even better
than before. I'll never really understand
that time of my life. But I believed. I think
G-d was pleased with that. I believed in
him even when things were grotty.

1. What was Job's life like before he started to suffer?

2. What horrible things happened to him?

3. Why did Job accept everything that was happening to him at first?

4. What reason did his friends give for his misfortunes?

5. Why did Job eventually get angry and rebel against G-d? What point was he trying to make?

6. Following this 'true story' in a magazine, readers wrote lots of letters about it. Split into two groups in class. Half should write the letters and half the replies. Make these into a letters page for the next edition of the magazine.

A Rabbi's view...

We asked Rabbi David Cohen to try to shed some light on what happened to Job:

In Job's day they believed that suffering was a punishment for sin – or sometimes even a warning about your bad behaviour, a kind of 'watch it or it'll get worse' idea. Job never really knew why he suffered or ever found out. So maybe that's not the point of his story. Maybe the point of Job's story is to tell us what to do when we suffer – how should we face up to it. Job got angry with G-d because he thought all his sufferings were unfair. But G-d answered his anger. So does Job's story tell us why we suffer? No, I don't think so. For me, the message is: Be patient with suffering as much as you can and live with it if you can. But if you do get angry about it (and you might), turn towards G-d. Too many people these days turn their anger towards other people. If suffering leads you to G-d then that's something at least. And just like Job, G-d will come to you. It's easy to believe in G-d when things are going well, but we need to believe when things are going badly too.

MAKING CONNECTIONS

❶ In groups, take a sheet of A3 paper and write in the centre 'The worst thing that has ever happened to me is...' Then around this write your own endings for the sentence.

❷ Job eventually got angry with G-d. What makes you angry? In what kind of situations is it right to be angry?

❸ Have you ever experienced something unpleasant which was a direct result of your actions? For example, getting a punishment exercise because of bad behaviour?

Thinking it over

❶ At first Job was patient and accepted everything that happened to him without complaining. Is patience always a good thing?

❷ What do you find difficult to accept about the world you live in? Why? What could you do to try to change it?

❸ Read the Rabbi's view. Write down in your own words the main point you think the Rabbi is trying to make.

❹ Do you think G-d's treatment of Job was fair? Why or why not?

❺ 'Suffering turned me away from G-d'. Why might a person say this?

❻ 'Suffering helped me find G-d'. Why might a person say this?

stimulus
4 Surviving suffering

The Bad Stuff	The Good Stuff	
Jews as slaves in Egypt. Treated very badly.	Eventually escape with G-d's help through Moses c.1400–1300.	
Temple destroyed and Jews exiled to Babylon c.587.	Returned by Edict of Cyrus and build 2nd Temple c.538.	
Conquered by the Greeks under Alexander the Great c.333.	The Jewish Maccabeans revolt and stir up hope of Jewish freedom.	
The Roman Empire takes over control of Israel ending in the destruction of the 2nd Temple in 70.	Jews continue to revolt against Roman rule, but many leave to spread all over Europe (the diaspora).	**BCE** / **CE**
Land of Israel changes hands many times – from Visigoths to Christians to Muslims – all have different approaches to the Jews still living there.	Judaism around Europe develops and changes, but survives.	
Christian crusaders capture Jerusalem in 1099. Recaptured by Muslim Saladin in 1187.	Jews better treated under Muslim rule than under Christian rule.	

Jews thrown out of England 1290, out of France 1306–94, out of Spain 1492, and out of Portugal 1496.	Jews continue to spread throughout the world keeping their faith and traditions alive. Arrived in New Amsterdam (New York) in 1654. The American and French revolutions in 1775 and 1789 mean new freedoms for Jews.	
Anti-Semitism rises in Europe. Jewish ghettoes set up. Pogroms in Russia and other Eastern European countries.	Jews move in great numbers around the world. Between 1881 and 1914, 2,750,000 Jews left Eastern Europe.	
The Holocaust. One third of all Jews in the world killed by the Nazis.	The Jewish faith survives – even in the concentration camps. The world begins to wonder if it is time to agree to a Jewish homeland.	
Many surrounding non-Jewish states pledge to get rid of Israel.	Declaration of the Independence of the State of Israel 1948.	

❶ Where were the Jews slaves?

❷ Who stirred up hope for Jewish freedom?

❸ What is the diaspora?

❹ Which two religions fought over Jerusalem for many years?

❺ What happened in America and France which led to new freedoms for Jews?

❻ What important event happened in 1948?

❼ Make your own timeline of Jewish history to go round your class. Include images and drawings as well as writing.

❽ Imagine you are a Jewish person living in a time of persecution. You can choose when this is, and you might need to do some more research into the topic. Write a letter to a friend in another country following this format:
   • Describe what life is like for you and what you are going through.
   • Describe how you manage to cope with the persecution.

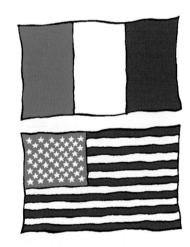

The Holocaust

Glasgow cleric, Ernest Levy, survived several concentration camps, including Auschwitz and Bergen-Belsen, two of the most heinous of those places where six million died. He remembers a young girl named Anne Frank. In 1945, her life was ended by disease in Belsen, just yards from Rabbi Levy's 'block'.

'She and I were in Belsen, yards from each other, at the same time.'

The retired rabbi added: 'I was older than she, and my dreadful duty was to drag thousands of dead, which would have included her, to be buried in a mass grave.

Faith is not something you think of then. It is a rock you climb on to later and realise that every new day is in itself a miracle'

www.news.scotsman.com

'I arrived in Auschwitz on 1 October 1944. I was about three months pregnant so it didn't show, and I was put among the strong people who could work. My son George's death from pneumonia, aged 2 months, in April 1944 saved my life, because if I had arrived with a baby I would have been sent straight to the gas chambers.

My husband was sent to Auschwitz three days before me and I never saw him again. After the war somebody told me point-blank: 'Don't wait for him, he was shot in front of me, for no good reason' (on 18 January 1945). The worst thing was the roll calls which lasted endlessly, and I fainted quite a few times, which was the worst thing you could do. But I had good friends who picked me up, because if I had been lying on the floor there was only one outcome. I remember the shouting and the dogs barking, and screaming and screaming and screaming.'

(Anka Bergman, 87, from Czechoslovakia, survived Auschwitz but lost her parents and siblings. In 1948 Anka started a new life in Cardiff. Her daughter Eva lives in Cambridge and works for the Holocaust Educational Trust – *The Observer*, 9 January 2005)

Jewish prisoners in a concentration camp

I have lived
dear G-d
in a world gone mad
and I have seen
evil
unleashed beyond reason or
understanding.

I was with them.
We drank from the same
bitter cup.

I hid with them
Feared with them,
Struggled with them
And when the killing was finally done
I had survived
while millions had died.
I do not know why

I have asked many questions
for which there are no answers
And I have even cursed
my life
thinking I could not
endure the pain.

But a flame
inside
refused to die.
I could not throw away
What had been ripped away
from so many.

In the end
I had to choose life.
I had to struggle to cross
the bridge between
the dead and the living.
I had to rebuild
what had been destroyed.
I had to deny death
Another victory.

Malka B
(www.remember.org)

❶ What was the 'daily duty' of Ernest Levy?

❷ What do you think Ernest Levy meant by 'every new day is in itself a miracle'? Design a poster based on this idea.

❸ Find out about the story of Anne Frank. See www.annefrank.org

❹ What factors helped Anka Bergman to survive Auschwitz?

❺ What answers do Jews give to the question of how they can continue to believe in G-d when faced with the suffering of the gas chamber?

Thinking it over

❶ What does it mean to have hope?

❷ Do you think there is hope in every situation, or are some situations hopeless?

❸ Is it possible to give people hope?

❹ 'The survival of the Jewish people proves that there must be a loving G-d.' Discuss the arguments for and against this statement.

❺ Do you think goodness will always win in the end? What makes you think this?

Tzedakah

Imagine a world where everyone had everything they needed. No one was hungry, no one was unfairly treated. Is such a world possible? What can be done to create a world more like that? This unit explores the Jewish idea of tzedakah which is about 'making the world a fairer place'. It looks at some of the ways in which charity is practised within Judaism and describes what the Jewish scriptures have to say about fairness and justice in everyday life.

IN THIS UNIT YOU WILL BE ASKED TO THINK ABOUT:

✓ CHARITY

✓ FAIRNESS

✓ JUSTICE

stimulus 1 *What is tzedakah?*

Tzedakah means charity, but it also means justice. Charity is where one person or group helps another. There are a number of ways of giving charity and helping people in need.

Money

You can give money – then people who need things can decide for themselves what to use the money for. You can give a lot of money or very little, but it all helps. You can do this by:

- putting money in a collecting can
- donating money on the Internet or on a phone-line
- writing a cheque at certain times of the year or in response to special appeals
- buying charity goods
- sponsoring something or someone
- having a set amount of money taken off your bank account every month.

Direct Aid

You can buy things to give directly to those who need them. For example:

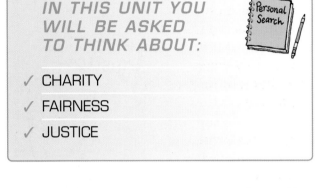

- books for schools
- food for the hungry
- medicines for those who are ill
- water pumps to provide clean water
- toys for needy children
- special equipment for special groups.

Practical Help

As well as giving money in one form or another, you can give charity by your actions. You could:

- visit people who are alone
- help out at a club for people with special needs
- do practical work, like helping people do their housework or going to developing countries and helping to build schools.
- offer the use of your skills for free.

Campaigning

Other kinds of action involve campaigning against the causes of injustice and unfairness. You could do this by:

- voting for one party as opposed to another at an election
- writing to your MSP/MP/MEP about injustice
- taking part in protests
- refusing to support places or products which might be linked with injustice or unfairness.

Jews and Tzedakah

> If … there is a fellow-Israelite in need, then do not be selfish and refuse to help him. Instead, be generous and lend him as much as he needs.
>
> (Deuteronomy 15:7–8)

Tzedakah is not a matter of choice – it is a duty. According to Jewish law, Jews are required to give 10% of their income to the poor. Jewish rabbis, however, have long taught that it is important to be sensible and that 5% is the maximum most people should give to avoid becoming poor themselves and being a further burden on the community.

In ancient times a box was placed at the back of the Temple into which people put their contributions. Today, Jewish families will have a tzedakah box into which they put money, particularly on the Sabbath and on festival days. When the box is full the money will be given to an organisation which helps those in need.

Gemilut Hassidim

The basis of the Jewish approach to charity and helping others is gemilut hassidim or loving-kindness. Practical help is not just helping the poor, it can be helping the rich too. It can be anything from visiting the sick to speaking kind words to someone. You can even carry out gemilut hassidim to the dead – by making sure that they have someone with them from their death until their burial.

> The world is sustained by three things; the study of the Torah, worship and gemilut hassidim.
>
> (Ethics of the Fathers)
>
> The world is judged with mercy and all is measured by the number of good deeds.
>
> (Ethics of the Fathers)

FINDING OUT

❶ What is tzedakah?

❷ What is a tzedakah box and how is it used?

❸ State two ways of giving money to charity.

❹ How can you campaign against injustice?

❺ What does Deuteronomy say about how Jews should respond to someone in need?

❻ What percentage of their income are Jews expected to give to the poor?

❼ What is gemilut hassidim?

❽ According to the Ethics of the Fathers what is the measure by which G-d judges everyone?

MAKING CONNECTIONS

❶ Do you know anyone who supports a charity or gives to good causes? Which charities do they give to? Do you give to any charities? Which ones? Carry out a class survey to see which charities, if any, are the most popular.

❷ What kind of charitable activities does your school get involved in? How successful have these been?

❸ What special skills do you think you could use for charity? Write them anonymously on a piece of paper and then place them secretly into a bag or box. Have them all read out in class. What range of skills are there in your class?

❹ Do one act of gemilut hassidim this week. You can either do this individually or in a group. Discuss your ideas and form a plan of action. Perhaps you could make this something you do more regularly.

stimulus 2 *Tzedek*

What is it?

Tzedek is a Jewish charity which puts tzedakah into action. Tzedek is a British charity founded in 1990. It aims to help people in need, wherever they are in the world. It doesn't matter what religion or race those in need are. It tries to help people to cope with their own situation and make them independent. It tries to keep projects small-scale so that there are clear benefits to the people in need.

What does it do?

It works to relieve as well as get rid of poverty. It helps community development – for example, water supply schemes. It helps in education and training and it helps communities make the most of what they have, whether it's agriculture or tourism. It helps financially through loan schemes and co-operatives.

What about those who receive charity?

Tzedek believes that those who receive charity should be helped in a way that shows respect and allows the recipient to retain their dignity. This is known as kavod. The aim is to do away with any need to give charity!

Here are just some of the projects Tzedek is involved in.

Project Title	Project Aim	Country	Year Tzedek Started Funding
Maternity Worldwide	Income generation and emergency maternity care fund	Ethiopia	2003
Sangbit	Mushroom growing cooperative funded via micro credit	India	2002
Borela Centre – Hope for Children (Handicapped, Orphaned, Poor and Exploited children)	Shelter for street kids	Sri Lanka	2002
Kumali Modern Preparatory School	School and community centre. Crafts sold for income generation	Uganda	2001
ERDS – Gajole Project	Micro credit scheme for rural women	India	2001
Ashram International – Milk Chilling – Kaliro Dairy Association	Farmers' cooperative milk packaging and marketing, plus housing improvement loans	Nepal	2001
www.tzedek.org.uk/overseas-projectlist-complete			

Some other Jewish Charities

Jerusalem Foundation
Jewish AIDS Trust
Jewish Blind & Disabled
Jewish Relief & Education Trust
Jewish Soup Kitchen
Jewish Women's Aid

Farming cooperative land

❶ Go to the Tzedek website if you can. Design an information leaflet about the organisation for people who have no access to the Internet.

❷ Find out about two other Jewish charities. Design an advert they might place in a Jewish newspaper.

MAKING CONNECTIONS

❶ Imagine you were going to start up a charity organisation. What would you want to support? How would you raise your money? What would you do? In groups, form a plan of action for your new charity. You should include the following items about your new charity: who you are, what you do, why you do it, how people can help? If you have computer skills you could design this as a mini website, otherwise you could design promotional materials, advertising posters etc.

❷ Choose one of the countries in the table and research the main problems that face the people there.

stimulus **3** *Rules about Tzedakah*

Certain ways of giving tzedakah are considered more deserving than others. Maimonides, a religious teacher who lived in the twelfth century, organised them into different levels. They are like the rungs of a ladder or steps, with the least deserving at the bottom and the most deserving at the top.

The Rules

- to help the poor to help themselves, by lending money or by providing work.
- to give and neither person knows who the other is
- to give, knowing who is going to receive the gift, but the receiver doesn't know who you are
- to give without knowing who is receiving your gift, but the receiver knows who you are
- to give before being asked
- to give but only after being asked to
- to give cheerfully but to give less than you should
- to give but in a grudging way

❶ Who was Maimonides?

❷ What does it mean to give 'in a grudging way'?

❸ Represent the rules of Maimonides in the form of a ladder or staircase starting with the least deserving at the bottom and rising to the most deserving at the top.

Thinking it over

❶ Why do you think the bottom rule of Maimonides is considered the least deserving while the top rule is the most deserving?

❷ Why might giving secretly be better for the giver than giving openly?

❸ Why might getting help secretly be better for the receiver than getting it openly?

❹ How should people decide which charities to support?

❺ Should people give on a regular basis or just when they feel like it?

❻ Should people only help others in their own town or country, or is it important to help people in other places as well? Why?

❼ Are there any benefits for the giver from giving to charity? Is it better to give or to receive?

❽ What's the real point of helping others?

❾ Some think that problems such as poverty and homelessness are 'nothing to do with me' What would you say?

❿ 'It is more important to give practical help than just to give money' What do you think?

4 *What does it mean to be fair?*

Is it fair that...

- Millions of children die each year of starvation or by drinking dirty water?
- There are still homeless people living on the streets of Scotland?

- People are sometimes attacked because of the colour of their skin?
- The poor are far more likely to get ill than the rich?
- Older people are often ignored by their families?
- Children are sometimes expected to act as carers even when this harms their education?

- Innocent people are killed in terrorist attacks around the world?
- Some footballers can earn more than a thousand pounds a week?
- Pop stars can earn millions each year by singing?
- Women still generally earn less than men – even when they're doing the same job?

Do not ill-treat foreigners who are living in your land. Treat them as you would a fellow-Israelite, and love them as you love yourselves. Remember that you were once foreigners in the land of Egypt.

(Leviticus 19:33–34)

If a fellow-Israelite living near you becomes poor and cannot support himself, you must provide for him as you would for a hired man, so that he can continue to live near you... Do not make him pay interest on the money you lend him, and do not make a profit on the food you sell him.

(Leviticus 25:35–37)

As a Jew, tzedakah for me is not about making me feel good. Nor is it just about money, it's a whole way of life. It's about the rights of others. It's about showing fairness to everyone, treating everyone as equals. It's about living life the way G-d intended us to live it.

(A Jewish believer)

❶ Using the Internet, newspapers and magazines, contribute to a classroom display labelled 'It's Not Fair'.

❷ Among the examples of unfairness you collected, are some kinds of unfairness more common than others? Why do you think this is?

❸ In groups make a list of jobs people do ranging from the everyday to things like movie actors and world leaders. For each one guess how much they earn in a year. Now do some research and find out how much people doing these jobs actually earn. What reasons are there for people in different jobs earning different amounts of money?

❹ What does the Book of Leviticus say about the treatment of foreigners? Why do you think it reminds Jews that they themselves were once foreigners?

❺ What does Leviticus teach about how to treat a fellow Israelite who is poor?

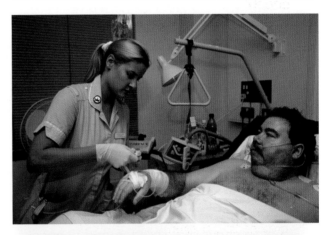

People earn different amounts for doing different jobs

MAKING CONNECTIONS

❶ Produce a list from your own experience of 'It's not fair' statements.

❷ Choose one of the statements from your list. What would you want to see happen to make things fairer?

❸ Are you always fair in your treatment of other people? Can you give examples?

❹ Have you ever treated someone unfairly, for example, accused someone of something only to find out later that you were wrong? How did you feel? What did you do to put things right?

❺ Imagine your school has been handed a gift of £10,000. Discuss and work out a fair way of dividing and using the money.

❻ What things are going on in the world which you could write to your MSP/MP/MEP about? Find an issue of fairness which concerns you and devise a letter. In the letter explain what you think is unfair about the situation and suggest what might be done to make things better. Perhaps you could send the letter – but let your teacher check it first!

Thinking it over

❶ From the work you have done so far, what do you think it means to be fair?

❷ Is it sometimes hard to be fair? Why is this?

❸ Does it matter whether you act fairly or not? Why or why not?

❹ What do we need to do to try and make sure that people act fairly?

❺ What is meant by 'fair play'? Give examples of what is fair and not fair in your favourite sport or game. Is it always clear what is fair and not fair? Why do you think this is?

stimulus **5**

More than just charity

Tzedakah means more than just charity. It is about justice.

> The world stands on three things: on justice, on truth and on peace.
> (Ethics of the Fathers)
>
> Tzedakah is equal to all the other commandments combined.
> (Talmud)
>
> Tzedakah is not about bestowing favours upon those less privileged than we are. It is about restoring the divine balance between the 'haves' and 'have-nots'. The widow, orphan and stranger must enjoy the same rights as everyone else. Tzedakah is the fulfilment of obligation.
> (Rabbi Hillel E. Silverman)

What tzedakah means for the Jewish Community Action organisation

- supporting the building of affordable housing
- investing in the community
- opposing gun violence
- supporting immigrants' rights
- opposing racism.

You can find out more about the work of the Jewish Community Action orgainisation by visiting www.jewishcommunityaction.org

A poor man borrowed a sum of money from a rich man. It was agreed that he would repay the loan in two weeks. Two weeks passed and the poor man could not repay it. The rich man took the poor man to court. The people of the town thought that, because the rich man was so wealthy, he should let the poor man off without paying him the debt he owed. When the matter came before the court the judge said that the poor man must repay what he owed. 'That is justice', he said. Then the judge took off his cap, turned it upside down and passed it round the crowd of townspeople. He told them all to reach into their pockets and help the poor man repay his debt. 'That is mercy', said the judge. (Adapted from *A Tapestry of Tales* – Sandra Palmer and Elizabeth Breuilly)

FINDING OUT

❶ According to the Talmud, how important is tzedakah?

❷ What is meant by the 'haves' and the 'have-nots'? Give examples.

❸ What are 'rights'? Give examples.

❹ What is this story trying to teach?

MAKING CONNECTIONS

❶ What obligations do you have at home, at school, in the wider community?

❷ Make a list of issues in your school or local community which you think need to be put right. Draw a circle with the word 'tzedakah' at the centre and add your ideas or images around this (for example, 'an end to bullying').

❸ Choose one of the issues that Jewish Community Action is concerned about. Draw up a plan of action showing how you might go about tackling it.

❹ In groups, prepare scripts for the characters in the story of the poor man and the judge. Then pull the parts together to act out the story.

Thinking it over

❶ What is justice? Is justice the same as being fair?

❷ When people say they want justice, what is it that they want?

❸ Choose one of the areas identified by the Jewish Community Action organisation. What might justice mean in relation it?

❹ The symbol for justice is a blindfolded person holding a pair of scales. Why do you think a pair of scales is used as a symbol of justice?

❺ Do you agree or disagree that justice and mercy must go hand in hand? Give reasons for your answer.

❻ 'School students don't have enough power to change the world'. What do you think?

Kashrut

We are more conscious about our diet today than ever before. We are often advised to cut out, or at least cut down on, 'fatty' foods and on the amount of sugar and salt we consume. The Jewish Bible, too, records certain dietary rules: animals, fish and birds that should not be eaten by the Jewish people. Jews call these regulations the Dietary Laws or, in Hebrew, kashrut. The things Jews can eat are kosher, meaning 'fit', and the things that are not fit for Jews to eat are terefah, meanng 'torn'.

> IN THIS UNIT YOU WILL BE ASKED TO THINK ABOUT:
>
> ✓ THE KILLING OF ANIMALS
> ✓ RULES
> ✓ CONTROL
> ✓ TRADITIONS

1 But it tastes nice!

Among the most popular foods that many people eat on a regular basis are the following:

Fish and chips
calories 1078
fat 65g
equivalent to 17
teaspoons of sugar
and ½ of a block
of lard

Pizza
calories 1746
fat 88g
equivalent to 31
teaspoons of sugar
and ⅓ of a block
of lard

Burger meal
calories 1300
fat 44g
equivalent to 38
teaspoons of
sugar and ⅕ of a
block of lard

Fried chicken
calories 933
fat 45g
equivalent to 14
teaspoons of sugar
and ⅕ of a
block of lard

The things we eat sometimes contain hidden ingredients. You might not mind these, or you just might not know about them…

Sometimes you really do not care what it is you eat
As long as it is tasty, spicy, tangy or just sweet
But hidden in those tasty morsels of delicious grub
Might just be stuff that you don't want to pass your slobbery gub.
Let's start with carmine, cochineal which makes your sweets bright red
It's beetle juice from ground up bugs – legs, body, eyes and head
Ice–cream and jelly such a treat, to make all children grin
But inside both might just be the dreaded gelatin
It's made from bones, from cartilage, tendons and pig skin
It's in your breakfast cereals and in your biscuit tin
And now a lovely chocolate bun, but so it isn't hard
Fat from piggies' abdomens or kidneys, yes it's lard.

Now what about that yummy cheese melting
on your toast
It got that way through rennet from a most
peculiar host
When you hear where it's from you might not
want to chuckle or to laugh
The slaughter house, the split wide open
stomach of a calf
Your chewing gum from lanolin – the wax on
a sheep's wool
The suet in your sticky pud – fat from a big
bull
The processed meat in burgers that make you
say yum yum
The meat in that, oh when you hear, will
make you really glum
They use it all, not much leftover, all fit to fill
your tum
Then butchers give it the almighty name of
'eyeballs, lips and bum'.

But don't stop there, so many things that you
would never dream
Your butter, milk, custard, yoghurt, spreads
and clotted cream
Might all be full of chemicals which keep the
milk-cow well
Until she's given all she can and barely fit to
sell
Then all those chemicals, poisons and stuff –
all that nasty goo
Will find its way, eventually, right inside you
And E numbers and additives, preservatives
and more
Not always made from animals, from grotty
things and gore
They'll maybe make you slightly odd and stifle
your ambition
Because they'll change your brain patterns and
give you a condition
But never mind, would you really care if you
were even eating mice
As long as it's yummy, hot and creamy, spicy
and tastes nice?
But think about what's in your nosh, eat but
use your head
'Cos maybe sooner than you think your food'll
make you dead!

MAKING CONNECTIONS

1 Write down three things you learned from the information in Stimulus 1.

2 Write down one thing that you eat which the poem said is full of something unusual.

3 Find out about E numbers in foods. What are they? Why are they used? In what way might they be harmful? See www.earthways.co.uk and look at their pages on danger foods.

4 In groups, make up food diaries for yesterday. Display and discuss these in class. How many of the things which you ate are 'bad' for you in some way?

5 Bring into class as many food labels as you can. Go through the list of ingredients on the labels and work out how many of them you really know anything about. You could present your findings in the form of graphs or tables as a display for other people in your school – perhaps you could put it in the school dining hall. If you like you could extend this by looking at other 'hidden' ingredients such as fats, sugar, salt, etc.

6 How much attention do you normally pay to what you eat?

7 If you knew what was in some things would you stop eating them?

8 Have you ever considered not eating some kinds of food? Why?

stimulus 2 *What is and isn't kosher*

The Lord spoke to Moses and Aaron, saying to them: Speak to the people of Israel, saying: From among all the land animals, these are the creatures that you may eat. Any animal that has divided hoofs and is cleft-footed and chews the cud – such you may eat. But among those that chew the cud or have divided hoofs, you shall not eat the following: the camel, for even though it chews the cud, it does not have divided hoofs; it is unclean for you… The hare, for even though it chews the cud, it does not have divided hoofs; it is unclean for you. The pig, for even though it has divided hoofs and is cleft-footed, it does not chew the cud; it is unclean for you. Of their flesh you shall not eat, and their carcasses you shall not touch; they are unclean for you. These you may eat, of all that are in the waters. Everything in the waters that has fins and scales, whether in the seas or in the streams – such you may eat.

(Leviticus 11:1–9)

A kosher kitchen

Although what is and what is not kosher is very complex the most important rules are:

- Only certain species of animal are permitted (for example, cows, sheep, chicken, fish) and other species (for example, pigs, rabbit, shellfish) are forbidden.
- When an animal is slaughtered, it must be killed very quickly and painlessly with a sharp blade. This is called shechitah and only a trained person (a shochet) is allowed to carry out the killing. So when visiting a restaurant not only would a Jew have to avoid the pork and the lobster on the menu, but they could not have the beef or the chicken either because it would not have been killed in a kosher manner.
- There can be no mixing of meat and dairy products at a meal. Nature creates milk to nourish the young and keep them alive. For Jews it is bad enough having to kill young animals for meat but to combine in any way the meat, with the milk produced by the mother, is even worse. As a result, Jews will not serve butter with a meal containing meat, or put cream in their coffee at such a meal. They will have separate sets of dishes and crockery for meat and non-meat meals.
- Jews are not allowed to eat blood (Leviticus 7:26). In order that all the blood is removed the Jewish butcher, or the person preparing the meal, will soak the meat in salted water for at least an hour. There are no special rules regarding fish.

❶ Explain in your own words the meaning of the following terms: kashrut, kosher, terefah, shechitah.

❷ What does the passage from Leviticus say about which animals are permitted and which are forbidden?

❸ Look up Leviticus chapter 11 and make two lists – one of animals which are kosher and one of those which are terefah. Include in your list reference to birds, insects and fish.

❹ Think about as many milk and meat combinations as you can. Make an A4 poster of these. You might like to look up some recipes in cookbooks in the library, or ask your Home Economics department for help. Some are more obvious than others (for example, cheeseburger). But remember the 'hidden' ingredients from the last stimulus!

❺ Why do many Jews eat vegetarian meals, especially when visiting a restaurant?

❻ You can buy special kosher foods ready-made. Go to your local supermarket and see if you can find any. Make a display of these in class (or look up www.greatfoodkosher.co.uk or www.buyjewishstuff.co.uk).

Thinking it over

❶ Jews regard shechitah as the most humane method of killing animals. Do you agree? Why or why not?

❷ How easy or difficult do you think it is for a Jewish family to keep the rules about food in today's world?

❸ Why do you think Jews believe it is important to keep their rules about food?

❹ 'Animals just exist for human use.' Do you agree? Why or why not?

stimulus

3 *Kashrut: a way of life*

Kosher isn't just about what you eat; it's a whole way of life. Some Jews observe it more strictly than others. What other things does kosher cover?

Kitchen design

A truly kosher kitchen will have separate areas for dealing with milk products or meat products. Different dishes will always be used for each. You might even have two sinks, one for meat and one for dairy. Restaurants that are kosher will have to have this. There has to be no chance of milk and meat products even coming close to each other.

Pets

Remember that kosher food doesn't just cover you, it covers your pets too.

Hanukkah Doggie treats from www.kosherpets.com

Clothing

Shatnez is the Jewish teaching that wool and linen should not be mixed in anything you wear. Jewish sources give no reason for this. There are laboratories which specialize in detecting whether something is shatnez or not.

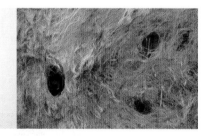

Linen and wool cannot be mixed

Kosher lifestyle

Whatever you do, you never know when it might not be kosher. To make sure that everything is really kosher, there are now kosher holiday companies, kosher cruises, kosher health farms. Sometimes whether it's kosher or not is something you wouldn't even think about – for example, did you

know that the glue used on Israeli stamps is certified kosher? Or that you can't eat crocodile because it's not kosher but you can wear crocodile-skin shoes?

Israeli postage stamps

MAKING CONNECTIONS

❶ Imagine you had to turn your kitchen into a kosher kitchen. Design a set of instructions about what has to change and why.

❷ Check the clothes you are wearing right now. Are they shatnez? Find an example of a shatnez piece of clothing and display it in your class. Surround it with notes explaining why it is shatnez.

❸ Look at some of the food labels you used in stimulus 1. Put them into categories as follows:
- completely non-kosher
- could be kosher
- kosher.

Remember to think carefully about the hidden ingredients inside the foods.

stimulus
4 *A young person's view*

Benjamin is a young Jewish boy. He describes why he follows the rules associated with kashrut.

Well, it's good because it makes you feel part of something bigger. I'm proud to be Jewish and I like to live a good Jewish life. A lot of people my age don't really care about anything very much even though they like to think they do. It's just TV and Playstations for them – they just shove any old food in their face without thinking about it. I'm sure if they were eating gerbils they wouldn't notice half the time! It makes me feel pleased with myself that I take a little time to think about what I eat and what I wear – but it doesn't all make me a dull guy you know. I've got loads of non-Jewish friends. We don't sit around all day comparing our religions – 'cos most of them don't have any religion anyway – well, maybe football. But that's their choice. Sometimes I do get a bit of humour from them about it, but it's never nasty. You know, like, 'Mmmm Ben, d'ye no fancy a wee bit of ma bacon roll, it's tasty'. To which I might reply, 'Aye great, and just dod a wee bit of vulture meat on top ae it as well will ye?' That makes everyone laugh. Sometimes they'll ask why I do it and sometimes they'll even listen to my answer. But they like the fact that we're all different – makes the world more interesting.

I've had my friends round to the house for dinner. They all enjoyed the food – 'It's just like normal food really isn't it?' they'd say. We're not as strict in our family as some, but that suits us fine. We think the rules about kosher are there to make our lives easier – not to get in the way of everything. Anyway, my Dad says if we're wrong, God will forgive us – we're only human after all! The only time it can be a bit annoying is when I'm out with my pals and we decide to go for a burger or something – but there's usually something I could eat. Maybe not something the Rabbi might exactly approve of, but I'm sticking fairly close to it all – anyway, who knows what's in half the food we buy. Keeping kosher as much as I can is my way of saying to the world, 'this is who I am'. Better than not thinking about it at all eh?

❶ What reasons does Benjamin give for following the rules about food?

❷ When is keeping kashrut sometimes difficult for Benjamin?

❸ What does Benjamin say about his family's attitude to the rules associated with kashrut?

MAKING CONNECTIONS

❶ Imagine you're going out with your pals to a fast-food place. Think about the menu and work out what Benjamin might be able to have.

❷ Do you know anyone who has had to follow a special diet? What? Why? How difficult was it for them?

❸ What rules are you expected to obey at home? Discuss your rules with others in a group and try to work out what lies behind the rules. Share your group's findings with the rest of the class and identify any common principles.

Thinking it over

❶ 'It's harder for a young Jew to follow religious rules about eating than for an adult.' Do you agree? Why or why not?

❷ Explain how Benjamin's friends made fun of him. Do you think people should make fun of people who have different beliefs and practices? Do you think Benjamin dealt with the situation in a good way?

❸ Do you agree with Benjamin that teenagers eat a lot of 'junk' without thinking about it? What do you think can be done to improve this situation?

stimulus
5 *What's involved in keeping kashrut?*

The following activity is intended to help you understand what's involved in observing kashrut. The principles represent the value or importance to Jews of keeping kashrut. The implications represent what Jews must do if they are to live up to the principles.

Principles

Keeping traditions alive	Standing up for your beliefs	Showing thoughtfulness in what you do
Being proud of your identity	Obeying the Torah (Law)	Showing concern for animals

Implications

Keeping kashrut means you do what your parents and grandparents before you have done.	If you keep kashrut you teach your children to carry this on when they are adults.	Kosher is the same today as it was in the past.	Keeping kashrut gives you a link with Jews throughout the ages.	You remember kosher rules from your childhood and you want your children to benefit.
Keeping kashrut means standing out from the crowd.	You might have to refuse to eat what your non-Jewish friends are eating.	People might laugh at or be annoyed by what they think is your fussiness.	You might have to say No! to an offer of food.	Every time you eat you show what you believe.
You don't just eat anything you're given.	At a restaurant you ask how the food was cooked.	You think about everything you eat.	You check the ingredients list carefully on foods that you buy.	You only buy foods from places you know are kosher.
Keeping kashrut shows that you are a Jew.	Following rules for eating shows that you are proud of who you are.	Keeping kashrut is a way of celebrating your faith.	You bring a packed lunch instead of eating school dinners, but you sit with non-Jewish friends to eat.	Keeping kashrut makes you 'different' but you're happy with that.
You follow the teachings in Leviticus.	The scriptures say you should eat only certain animals.	All plants are kosher according to the Torah.	You eat only what the Law allows.	You read your holy book and follow its teachings about food.
Shechitah is a kind way to kill animals for food.	By not eating milk and meat together you don't 'Cook the calf in its mother's milk'.	Shechitah is fast and painless for the animal.	You are less likely to eat animals which have been treated badly during their life.	You don't eat animals which have died from disease.

There is nothing particularly wicked about eating pork or lobster, and there is nothing particularly moral about eating cheese or chicken instead. But what the Jewish way of life does by imposing rules on our eating is to take the most common and ordinary activity and give it deeper meaning, turning it into an occasion for obeying (or disobeying G-d). If a non-Jew walks into a fast-food establishment and orders a cheeseburger, he is just having lunch. But if a Jew does the same thing, he is making a religious statement. He is declaring that he does not accept the rules of the Jewish dietary system as binding upon him. The rules lift the act of having lunch out of the ordinary and make it a religious matter. If you can do that to the process of eating, you have done something important.

(Adapted from *To Life: A Celebration of Jewish Being and Thinking* – Rabbi Harold Kushner)

According to Rabbi Harold Kushner there is nothing really wrong with pork and right with chicken. Dietary laws, he says, have the effect of turning eating into a religious activity. The reason for observing kashrut is not hygiene but love of G-d. G-d has said that we should try to control our appetite for food. By learning how to control our appetite for food, we train ourselves to control our appetite for other things.

FINDING OUT

❶ By talking to others in your group identify the implications that relate to each principle. Record your decisions.

❷ Which principle do you think would be most difficult to live up to? Why?

❸ What do you understand by traditions?

❹ According to Rabbi Harold Kushner, why do Jews observe kashrut?

MAKING CONNECTIONS

❶ If someone asked you to describe your 'traditions', what would you say? Are your traditions associated with your family, the wider community, Scotland as a whole? Discuss your answers in groups and with the whole class to see if there are traditions that everyone holds in common.

❷ How well do you control your appetite for material things – new clothes, CDs, DVDs the latest mobile phone? Do you give your parents a hard time if you don't get them?

❸ Have you ever felt that you have lost control of a situation and didn't know what to do? What happened?

❹ What things do you most need to control in your life? How successful are you in controlling them?

Thinking it over

1 How important is it to follow the traditions of your family or religion? Is it also important to make up your own mind about how to act and what to believe? Are the two things likely to come into conflict? What might happen as a result?

2 'Thinking carefully about what you eat will make you a better person.' What do you think of this statement?

3 Is it important for people to control their appetite for material things? Why or why not?

4 Do you think you have enough control over how you live your life? What makes you say that?

5 Are young people given too much say over what they do and where they go? Why do you think that?

6 Keeping traditions helps people have a better and more controlled life. Do you agree? Why or why not?

Index